Judith R.: "When I would come home from parties, never having met a man because of my weight, I would head straight for the refrigerator to console myself."

Ellin: "There were about five or six delicatessens near where I lived, and usually I would stop at all of them, buying something different so it wouldn't look so bad. I usually would try to buy something normal, like bananas or chicken, along with the ice cream, the cookies and the candy."

Diane James: ". . . I feel at least I'm selfishly enjoying something . . . You can be thin and please your boyfriend and be starved, or you can please yourself."

TRUE STORIES FROM
SUCH A PRETTY F...

"Any woma̲... ...weight— whether it wa̲... ...nds, or the first fifty—will be gr̲... ...jul and dignified book."

—Gloria Steinem

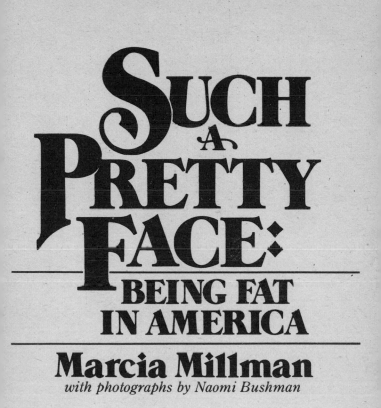

SUCH A PRETTY FACE:
BEING FAT IN AMERICA

Marcia Millman

with photographs by Naomi Bushman

BERKLEY BOOKS, NEW YORK

This Berkley book contains the complete
text of the original hardcover edition.
It has been completely reset in a type face
designed for easy reading, and was printed
from new film.

SUCH A PRETTY FACE:
Being Fat in America

A Berkley Book / published by arrangement with
W. W. Norton and Company

PRINTING HISTORY
Norton edition / February 1980
Berkley edition / June 1981

ISBN: 0-425-04849-7

A BERKLEY BOOK ® TM 757,375
Berkley Books are published by Berkley Publishing Corporation,
200 Madison Avenue, New York, New York 10016.
PRINTED IN THE UNITED STATES OF AMERICA

Grateful acknowledgment is extended to the following for permission to reprint copyrighted material:

Excerpts from *Lady Oracle* by Margaret Atwood
Copyright © 1976 by Margaret Atwood
Reprinted by permission of Simon & Schuster, a Division of Gulf & Western Corporation.

Excerpt from "Walking Into The Fire: Sarah Caldwell Comes To The Met," by Robert Jones. *Opera News* vol. 40, no. 14 (February 14, 1976), pp. 11–12.
Copyright © 1976 by the Metropolitan Opera Guild Inc.
Reprinted with permission of *Opera News*, published by the Metropolitan Opera Guild.

Excerpt from "Deviance Avowal in Daily Interactions Between Overweights and Thin Normals," by Natalie Allon
Presented at the meetings of the Society for the Study of Social Problems, 1976.
Reprinted with permission of Natalie Allon.

Excerpt from "Looksism As Social Control," by Gudrun Fonfa.
Lesbian Tide (January 1975), p. 20.
Copyright © 1975 by Tide Publications
Reprinted by permission of *Lesbian Tide*, a Tide Publication.

Excerpt from "Fat Dykes Don't Make It," by Lyn Mabel-Lois.
Lesbian Tide (October 1974), p. 11.
Copyright © 1974 by Tide Publications
Reprinted by permission of *Lesbian Tide*, a Tide Publication.

Acknowledgments

Throughout the three years that it took to complete this book, Naomi Bushman was the best collaborator and comrade that one could hope to find. She was a partner not only as a photographer but in every aspect of thinking through and completing the work.

Alexandra Botwin told me about some of the psychological defenses and syndromes she has observed in overweight women. She deserves a great deal of credit for many of the central ideas in the book.

B. K. Moran played a critical role in helping me to clarify, refine, and organize my thoughts and my writing. Her tough but constructive criticism and her constant support and good judgment steered me through many problems.

Edwin Barber provided exceptionally wise and generous editorial advice and helped me enormously in sharpening and focusing the writing. His encouragement and faith in the book were sustaining forces in the course of revising the manuscript.

Nancy Adler, Natalie Allon, Bernie Beck, John Brockman, Joan Chodorow, Fletcher Copp, Arlene Kaplan Daniels, Elissa E. Epel, Ella Hurst, John Kitsuse, Gerald M. Platt, Leonard Ross, Syrl Silberman, Philip E. Slater, Barrie Thorne, and Norma Juliet Wikler all helped in significant ways. Kathie Castro, Shelley Starr, and Betsy Wootten provided thoughtful and excellent secretarial assistance.

I would also like to thank the Faculty Research Committee and the Division of Social Sciences of the University of California at Santa Cruz for financial assistance.

Finally, I am deeply grateful to everyone who appears in this book, for all of them gave generously of their emotions, spirit, and time. It was their hope, as well as mine, that bringing these often painful experiences into the open might offer insight and reassurance to other people.

For Alexandra Botwin

Contents

Preface

Most books about obesity consist of techniques for losing weight, or treat weight as a physical phenomenon. The argument of this book is that the effort to lose weight should be secondary to the effort to understand the meanings of being overweight. These meanings are everywhere in the society at large and in the individuals who consider themselves, or are considered by others, to have a weight problem. What it means to be fat, beyond the purely physical experience of weighing any particular number of pounds, often shapes the identities and lives of fat people. And because obesity is so dreaded and laden with interpretations, many who are not actually overweight (especially women) may nonetheless suffer enormously because they wish they were thinner.

What is it like to live as a fat person in our society, at a time when obesity and fat people are increasingly disparaged? How does being overweight come to dominate a person's social identity and self-concept? How may people use being fat to express something about themselves and their place in the world? Does weight have a different significance for women than for men? These are among the questions this book explores. The material is drawn from long interviews with people who are overweight or concerned about their weight, as well as my observations of various organizations of overweight people, ranging from a politically oriented "fat rights" organization to Overeaters Anonymous, a society of people trying to reform themselves.

Although I describe some characteristic ways of viewing the world and living in it that are prominent in the biographies of fat people, I would not say that any special type of personality characterizes overweight people. The reasons for getting or staying fat vary widely and cannot be reduced to simple formulas or explanations. But because overweight people in America share a visible characteristic that is highly stigmatized they also tend to share the experience of making a personal career out of being fat. By "career" I mean that people organize their lives around situations other than their occupations. Being fat, like having a work career, is something that is experienced over time. It has its routines and expectations, its characteristic ups and downs; it has its crises, adventures, romances, panics, depressions, and rewards. People who are otherwise different but alike in being fat therefore often build a life in similar ways.

Although the book is specifically about the lives of fat people, it is also about more universal life experiences: for example, how people account for suffering and disappointment with personal and psychological explanations as opposed to social and political ones, and how they make connections between the two. It is also about the kinds of relationships that women of all sizes have with their bodies, and how women use their bodies to express conflicts about sex roles and their place in the world. It is about the universal experience of seeking or undergoing a significant physical or personal transformation and therefore of encountering dramatic discontinuities in one's life. Finally, it is about the experiences we undergo as we attempt to change ourselves or struggle to achieve a measure of self-acceptance.

The negative reactions and anxieties aroused by obesity cannot be adequately explained by the argument that obesity is unhealthy. Many other things we do to ourselves are unhealthy, yet they do not incite the same kind of shame, hostility, and disapproval. Furthermore, many people have strong reactions to weight even when a person is not fat enough for health to be affected.

Clearly, obesity has become mythologized in our culture into something much more than a physical condition or a potential health hazard. Being overweight is now imbued with powerful symbolic and psychological meanings that deeply affect the person's identity in the world. In other words, the state of being fat is felt to express something basic about a person's character and personality.[1]

And it is especially the case that an overweight woman is assumed to have a personal problem. She is stereotypically viewed as unfeminine, in flight from sexuality, antisocial, out of control, hostile, aggressive. One of the reasons for this assumption is that despite all the gains and insights of the women's liberation movement, women are still judged very much on the basis of physical appearance. And no matter what medical evidence we acquire to the contrary, being overweight is fundamentally viewed as an *intentional* act. In the case of women, being fat is considered such an obvious default or rebellion against being feminine that it is treated as a very significant, representative, and threatening characteristic of the individual.

There are several reasons why gaining insight into the social and psychological meanings of obesity is more important than learning any particular technique for losing weight. It has been repeatedly documented that almost all diets fail in the long run: no matter what reducing method is used, weight losses are maintained for at least two years in only five to ten percent of the cases. If being thin were simply a matter of acquiring the right eating and exercise habits, surely more people would find a way to stay thin. Obviously there are other reasons why people typically regain lost weight. But, more importantly, whether being fat is really a symptom of underlying emotional conflicts or simply the logical outcome of bad eating habits or a particular body type, the overweight individual, especially if she is a woman, probably suffers more from the social and psychological stigma attached to obesity than she does from the actual physical condition. In a wide variety of ways she is negatively defined by her weight and excluded from full participation in the ranks of the normal.[2]

Under these circumstances, the almost exclusive focus placed on dieting as the automatic solution to weight problems really overlooks more enduring and significant questions about the subject. Although there is increasing concern that obesity is a national disease of epidemic proportions (according to commonly used criteria, about 40 percent of the adult American population could be considered significantly overweight—that is, at least 20 percent above their "ideal" weight), and although dieting is a topic of endless conversation and the organizing principle for a multibillion-dollar industry, we seldom encounter a really serious discussion of the powerful feelings that fatness arouses in us, nor any thoughtful exploration of why fat people are so stigmatized and excluded. There is something dreaded, forbidden, taboo about the subject. Several of the people I interviewed for this book jokingly suggested that obesity is for us what sexuality was for the Victorians. The comparison is worth making, for as the stories in this book tell us, obesity arouses emotions of surprising intensity, including horror, contempt, morbid fascination, shame, and moral outrage.

This book is the product of my professional research as a sociologist, yet my original motive for the study sprang out of a personal interest as well. I have been successful at many things in my life, including completing projects that took several years of considerable and sustained efforts, yet I have at times felt tremendously frustrated and foiled at being unable to lose twenty pounds. And although I am tough and take pleasure in a good fight with a formidable opponent, on occasion I have actually dissolved into tears when someone suggested that I should be on a diet.

Before starting this research I had experienced many conflicting thoughts and feelings about weight. Since my own weight has fluctuated, I know from experience that the world is kinder to a slim woman. On the one hand, it seemed silly to allow weight to cause me such distress, yet I also deeply resented what seemed an arbitrary and oppressive standard of normal weight and of what is acceptable and attractive in a woman. Something in me balked at conforming to the demand, though I knew my life would be easier if I did. My dilemma is shared by many other women; the conflict I experienced was related to other kinds of pressures and unsatisfactory choices that women face in many other areas of life. But curiously, feminist writers and speakers, while calling attention to the pain and wasted human talent and energy that are produced in our society by the stress on physical beauty or the absence of it, have rarely dealt with the anxiety that women have about getting fat, or the self-hatred and shame they feel if they are overweight.

Having said something about what this book is, I want to say what it is not. First, when I talk about the meanings and characteristic experiences of being overweight, I am talking specifically of these in the context of contemporary, white, middle-class, urban American culture. I would not claim, for example, that my discussion is valid for rural, southern black women, since until recently women with substantial bodies have been considered attractive in the black community.

Second, I do not dwell on the medical or physiological aspects of obesity. Others have already written on this subject. I would, however, like to say a few things about obesity as a health problem in order to clarify the starting points of this analysis.

When asked to consider the fact that overweight people are badly treated in our society, people often respond by saying, "But you can't deny that being fat is unhealthy." One need not deny that obesity may be unhealthy to ask why fat people are so stigmatized; people with other health problems are not condemned in the same ways. Many people who are not overweight enough to be at a health risk still suffer great diminution in the quality of their lives because of the negative interpretations attached to being overweight, and many do more harm to their health by using dangerous drugs and diets trying to reach an unrealistically thin ideal. Since physical appearance rather than health is often the motivating factor in why and how people diet, and since many suffer more from the social stigma of being overweight than from the health hazards, it should be obvious that the problem of obesity and the solutions to it involve more than medical considerations.

When I compare Naomi Bushman's photographs with what I have written, I often think she and I emphasized different sides of being overweight. The photographs tell us a great deal about the social persona of each subject. The face and the body that are presented to the camera and to the photographer are the face and body that are presented to the world: sometimes proud, sometimes defiant, sometimes ingratiating, sometimes self-deprecating. In looking at the photographs we see how a person who is self-conscious about her looks holds herself together as she faces the world and those who judge her.

The subjects' autobiographical stories, on the other hand, reflect a private expression. On the whole, the personal accounts reveal vulnerabilities and sadness that are not admitted as directly by the photographed subjects who smile and pose with pride. (There is no correspondence between the subjects of the photographs and the accompanying quoted captions, since we wished to preserve the anonymity of the speakers.) Perhaps one of the reasons for the difference is that in the stories, unlike the photographs, the subjects are blanketed by anonymity, for I always stated at the outset that I would not use real names. Perhaps it mattered that I could identify myself as a person with a weight problem, whereas Naomi Bushman, being slender, could not. Yet despite these differences I would not say that either portrait or verbal expression is more honest, for how a person presents herself to the world and what she thinks of herself in private are equally profound aspects of her identity.

Marcia Millman

San Francisco, California
May 1979

ONE

❧❦

The
Social Worlds
of
Fat People

1

NAAFA: It's All Right to be Fat

Under flashing strobe lights, flesh undulates in all directions. The dance floor is filled with monumental women, women who weigh 250, 300, 400 pounds and more. They are spectacularly dressed in sexy, bare-cut evening gowns that are designed to display rather than cover the body. Necklines plunge. Some gowns are backless. Some have sequins or feathers or spaghetti straps.

The women are members of the New York City chapter of the National Association to Aid Fat Americans (NAAFA). Many have come to this dance hoping to meet a man who might love them despite their weight. In fact, the dance has attracted men who are especially drawn to fat women.

Alongside the walls slim men stand motionless and silent in their dark business suits. Some have come to a NAAFA dance for the first time after reading an ad in the *Village Voice*. A few are veterans of these dances and have dated several of the women who are present. Some are regular members of the organization and identify themselves as fat admirers—men who have a sexual preference for fat women. By late in the evening a few new couples are embracing passionately. But there are also several men who remain quietly on the sidelines, frankly staring at the women who are gathered in small groups. It is the largest women who are most hotly pursued—those who weigh under 250 pounds are seemingly at a disadvantage.

Despite its emphasis on social activities such as this dance,

NAAFA is also a political organization with a few dozen chapters in cities across the United States. It was started in 1969 by an average-sized electrical engineer from New York who had not only observed the suffering of his large wife but had experienced at first hand the embarrassment and difficulties of being a man who is attracted to fat women. In addition to providing fat people and fat admirers a comfortable refuge in a hostile world, NAAFA offers its members and the public a perspective on obesity that runs against the grain of almost all commonly held attitudes and conceptions about being fat.

The organization asserts that fat can be beautiful and that going on a diet is not always the solution to a fat person's problems. Instead, it stresses how fat people and fat admirers are victims of prejudice, stigma, and consequent self-hatred. NAAFA's purpose is to call attention to the exclusion, exploitation, and psychological oppression of fat people and to press for changes in the ways fat people are regarded and treated. Its central message is that it's all right to be fat.

In their efforts to demonstrate how they are victimized, NAAFA members point out the problems fat Americans encounter in daily life such as difficulty buying nice clothes, job discrimination, social exclusion, personal shame and low self-esteem, exploitation by commercial interests, inability to buy most health and life insurance, unsympathetic treatment by doctors, public ridicule. They argue that being fat is not always caused by a lack of will power but that body type, heredity, early childhood habits, and metabolism contribute to obesity. NAAFA also takes the position that the so-called negative effects of overweight on health have been enormously exaggerated, and that a too-high weight for one person may be normal for another. Even though NAAFA concedes that weight loss might be desirable for health reasons, its members argue that the typical experience of many fat people of repeatedly losing and regaining weight may be more destructive than maintaining a stable high weight. Thus a central goal of the organization is to help fat people accept and respect themselves as they are to live the fullest and happiest lives possible.

The organization does not discourage dieting. Even though the fat admirers in NAAFA are attracted to fleshy bodies, it would be misleading to say that the women in NAAFA are glad to be overweight. Most have come to NAAFA because they are at the end of the conventional line—having repeatedly

failed to become and stay thin, they've decided to learn to live with what they are. Being unable to pass for normal in the outside world, they have found a comfortable home among their own.

Because most of the members of NAAFA have had trouble meeting social and sexual partners through conventional sources, they are partly attracted to the organization's match-dating service and its dances. There is also a newsletter published every few months with useful information: reviews of medical treatments dealing with weight (for example, a series of articles on the hazards of intestinal bypass surgery), advice about how and where to buy large clothes or find wide seats in airplanes and theaters, names of physicians recommended as not hostile to fat people, reviews of books about dieting and weight, items about discrimination in employment, and announcements of weddings between members who met through the organization. NAAFA also engages in public demonstrations, letter-writing campaigns, and interviews with the media to call attention to activities and policies that are discriminatory, demeaning, or offensive to fat people.

Several of the most active members of this NAAFA chapter are young, single, and very large. Laura Campbell, for example, is big even by NAAFA standards. She weighed as much as 450 pounds, and although she recently lost 75 pounds her weight is once again approaching its previous high. Laura, who is twenty-eight years old, works as a secretary in a banking corporation in New York City. Like many other members of NAAFA she invests considerable effort in having stylish clothes made to order—both her work outfits and the gowns she wears to NAAFA dances. Her hair is always cut in high-fashion styles, and in public situations she is careful about her attire. But interviewed at home late one evening, she wore only a loose housecoat, exhibiting a lack of guardedness that is remarkable considering the assaults she has sustained in her lifetime. Since she was a child, Laura has known what it is like to live in the world as a freak, and to be treated as a curiosity in the streets, in stores and in her own family. In the interview that follows, she describes how her life was changed by joining NAAFA.

Laura Campbell

People are always making loud remarks about me in the street, like, "Look at that woman. She should be in a circus," or, "Look at that fat elephant."

One day I was in the supermarket and a four-year-old kid was marching around and around me in circles, screaming at the top of his lungs, *"You are fat. You are fat. You are fat"*—over and over again. I wanted to choke that kid, or say to his mother, "You should teach your child some manners." But it's complicated. Sometimes children are only stating a fact, and by saying they shouldn't say it, it's like agreeing that being fat is bad.

Once I was visiting a cousin of mine, and we were sitting at a table, and her little boy was crawling underneath. He came out and said, "Boy, you have the fattest legs I ever saw." My cousin started hitting him, and he asked, "Why are you hitting me? Was that a bad thing to say?"

People often stop me in the street and say, "You have such a pretty face. Why don't you try Weight Watchers?" Once a woman stopped me in the street and said, "I have a fabulous doctor you could go to."

Or often at family parties a relative will corner me and say, "So what are you doing about your weight? I hate to see you this way." When that happens my whole evening is ruined. I used to answer my relatives by saying "I know, you're right." But now I tell them my doctor told me not to diet until I'm ready to lose all the weight and keep it off because its unhealthy to keep losing and gaining.

A client came into the office to discuss some business with me, and when we were finished she said, "So what's the matter with you? Do you have gland trouble?"

It's amazing how insensitive people can be to fat people. You wouldn't walk up to a cripple in the street and say, "How did you lose the use of your legs?" So I don't know why people think it's all right to say these things to us.

I have several friends who are teachers and are fat, and they have a problem disciplining the children. If you're fat, they don't feel you're an authoritative figure. It's especially hard for women. A fat man could be seen as aggressive, but a fat woman is just seen as a pushover.

My family has only come to accept me the way I am in the last few years. I remember sitting on a stool in the Chubby Department of Lane Bryant when I was seven years old and my mother screaming at me that I had outgrown the biggest chubby size and she could kill me because now at the age of seven she'd have to get me clothes in women's sizes.

My mother was always thin and had twenty-five boyfriends when she was young, and she wanted the same thing for me. Most mothers think of daughters as extensions of themselves, and it really drove her crazy that I was fat. When I was ten years old they put me on diet pills—about nine a day. They were amphetamines and I was miserable. I couldn't sleep, and I was so nervous I was half out of my mind, but my parents didn't think there was anything wrong with the pills. I was closer to my father. In fact I hated my mother from the time I was thirteen to eighteen. When I was a teenager my mother told me, "Look how fat you are. Even your father said he thinks you're getting repulsive." I screamed back at her, "He didn't say that!" But I believed her, and it hurt me so much because I loved my father. After my mother told me that, I avoided my father for years afterwards and didn't talk to him, and I never asked him about it. Now when I think about it I'm not sure he ever said such a thing to her—she may have said it to frighten me into dieting. And if I asked her now if it were true, she probably wouldn't remember.

My mother wanted me to be like her—the belle of the ball. She's reliving her life through my younger sister. Her behavior toward me still hurts, even now. To my sister she'll say, "Oh, you look beautiful. Where did you get that dress?" And to me all she'll say is "Where'd you get *that?*"

I've been to diet doctors, Weight Watchers, Weigh of Life. I've had shots and diet pills and I've lost weight many times and gained it back. My family has spent thousands of dollars getting me to lose weight, and it's only in the last few years that they've accepted me.

Before I joined NAAFA I was really socially backward. I never dated. I just stayed home and watched TV. My mother told me I would never have a boyfriend.

When I first started dating men I was very embarrassed for the man and didn't want to go out of the house. I'd say, "I'll make dinner," or, "Let's watch TV." Once I went to the movies on a date and some kids said, "Look at that man with that fat woman." One of the men I knew insisted we go out, but I was terrified of walking by some teenagers. I would rather have walked on hot coals to California. I wanted to let the man walk in front of me so if the kids made any remarks to me, he wouldn't hear.

Before I joined NAAFA I used to deny my situation—like I would try to squeeze and squeeze through the turnstile in the subway even though I couldn't fit, probably attracting *more* attention that way. Now I pay the fare and walk through the gate instead, and even though I have to acknowledge I'm too big for the turnstile, I probably attract less attention.

I've met boyfriends in NAAFA but the men there are often like roosters in a hen house. There are a lot more women than men and the men work their way around to all of the women and the organization happens to be very gossipy. I might mention that So-and-So called me up, and someone will say, "Oh, don't bother with him. He's cheap." Or they'll tell me he only wants to go to bed with a woman. So, you sort of know about everyone already, even before you meet them.

What I really like about the organization is that we talk about what makes us unhappy—the people in NAAFA are very caring. You can always pick up the phone and call someone when you're feeling depressed. NAAFA allows us to be comfortable being ourselves. People wear outrageous, revealing clothes to NAAFA meetings but most of us wouldn't wear them on the outside. I'm pretty outgoing in NAAFA but outside I'm pretty retiring. I didn't go to the beach until this year but my boyfriend encouraged me to go and to wear a bikini. I had a black satin bikini made but I didn't feel comfortable. I don't really think fat is that attractive to look at.

Usually at an NAAFA dance, I'll dance up a storm but I didn't feel like dancing in front of some of the reporters that came to the last dance. I get the feeling that some of them don't take the organization seriously. And most of them don't talk to us—they just stare at us dancing. You're not gonna get to know people by just looking at them—all you'll see is the fat. For example, at the lunch buffet at our convention last year there was a reporter sneaking behind me to see how much I put on my plate—how many sandwiches I was eating.

Being in NAAFA has helped me not to cringe at the word *fat*, and it's made me more comfortable talking about it. Before, if someone near me would discuss weight I'd leave the room because I'd be afraid they'd ask me how much I weigh. I used to lie when people asked me how much I weigh. They expect you to be embarrassed or to try to get out of answering. I don't like it when people are indirect. They ask you, "How much would you like to lose?" And then they ask, "What weight would you be down to then?" So now I say, "If you really want to know how much I weigh, I'll tell you." After I say that, people often protest, "Oh no. I was just wondering how much you want to lose." I used to lie when I told how much I weighed—I'd take off 30 pounds. But now I tell the truth.

I can tell by how I feel trying to walk that my weight is going up again. I had gotten down to 375 and it bothers me to think of being in the 400s again. The 400s are upsetting to me as a category. In NAAFA we don't compete about weight—it would be considered in bad taste to comment negatively about each other's appearance. So no one says anything critical to me, but I think to myself, NAAFA is supposed to be for fat people and I'm the largest one at meetings, so what does that make me? Or Lane Bryant is supposed to be for fat people, and I can't fit into their clothes, so what does that make me?

In NAAFA I've learned how to live with being fat. I discovered I could have a boyfriend and move away from my parents and get my own apartment. But I'm not happy about it. Most of the people in NAAFA are not really happy—we would prefer to be thin if we could but NAAFA has helped me to learn how to manage.

Rhetta Moskowitz is an imposing woman with a booming voice and long, black frizzy hair worn loose. She is five feet, six inches tall and weighs well over 300 pounds. She enjoys her reputation of being outrageous and intimidating, and being even more assertive about fat liberation than most other NAAFA members, she wears revealing clothes even outside NAAFA events.

Rhetta lives in a tiny tenement apartment in Brooklyn. The walls are painted black and decorated with sculptures made from the styrofoam packing molds for stereo components. She has had many different jobs, most recently having worked as a bookkeeper. Although her father is a physics professor and she grew up in an academic environment, she is starting college only now at the age of thirty-three.

During the interview Rhetta Moskowitz lounged on her kingsize bed which filled the one-room apartment. As we started to talk she apologized for having been abrupt on the phone earlier that afternoon, explaining that she had been in the middle of making love when I called. In our conversation, she drew a comparison between the experiences of NAAFA members with people in other stigmatized categories, and talked about the process of learning to be comfortable with one's body.

Rhetta Moskowitz

In terms of discrimination, the best equivalent of being fat is being a homosexual. For years the NAAFA mailings were sent out in plain brown wrappers because people were ashamed to have anyone see they belonged, especially the fat admirers. There is such a thing as a closet fat person or a closet fat admirer. And other people put fat people in the closet. They don't talk about it and don't acknowledge it. No one will use the word *fat* in front of you. They use circumlocution, like *zoftig* or *heavy*, or say that you have a pretty face.

I had a child when I was young, and during the last

part of my pregnancy I was sent to a home for unwed mothers. I noticed that when girls first came to the home they covered their bodies, but after a few days they let their stomachs pop out. It's the same in NAAFA—after coming to a few meetings people stop holding in their flesh and relax about their bodies. In NAAFA you get used to hearing the word *fat*, and you stop being competitive about who's fat and who's thin.

I heard about NAAFA from a man I was going with. I met him through an ad in the *Village Voice*. All my life I've been called Mama Cass by people in the street. Meanwhile, I was sharing an apartment with a friend who told me that I wouldn't believe an ad in the *Village Voice* that said, "Man seeks Mama-Cass type woman." I wrote him a letter, and he called me up, and he sounded interesting on the phone, so we went out. He told me what it was like to be a man who liked fat women and I decided on that basis to join NAAFA.

I once put an ad in the Village Voice myself. I used the term *zoftig* and got over five hundred calls. About 20 percent of the callers didn't know what *zoftig* was. I got calls from all over the country and decided to meet about fifty people. Five of them are still friends.

I went through years of therapy but didn't come to terms with being fat. I was really helped more by a man who I liked a lot who told me I turned him on. And in NAAFA people learn to like themselves more and to be less anxious.

Another member of the New York chapter of NAAFA, Gloria Cohen, talked about how the organization rescued her from a life of social isolation. Gloria recalled that being fat really affected her life only after she got to high school and girls started to have women's shapes and be interested in boys. At this point, Gloria realized that she wasn't being treated the same way as the rest of the girls.

When she was fifteen she spent a year living in a hospital and participating in a research project on obesity. During that year she got to know fellow patients with serious diseases such as polio, multiple sclerosis, and spinal deformities. In the special world of the hospital Gloria got involved with other people and activities for the first time. To each other they were all "regular" people. Some of her new friends died during that year. Leaving the hospital she felt much older than other sixteen-year-old girls, and she decided she couldn't go back to high school. Instead, she took a speedwriting and typing course so she could get a job. Soon after that, Gloria's mother died and her only sister got married, so Gloria was left alone. Her story illustrates how NAAFA often draws people out of a solitary life.

Gloria Cohen

When my sister got married I had no friends, and I told myself whatever link I had with humanity is gone. I used to come home from work on Friday afternoon and pull up a chair in front of my TV and line up the food next to me, and that was it until I went back to work on Monday. I functioned all right during work hours, but when I came home I would sit or sleep in my chair and paint paint-by-number pictures of animals by the hundreds. My sister thought this was an unhealthy way to live and sent me to a psychiatrist, but I hated him from the start.

One day my brother-in-law was shaving and listening to the radio and heard the end of an interview with a member of NAAFA. He called me up and said, "Gloria, do I have a club for you—there's a club where guys like fat girls." I wrote to the address he had heard, and I joined in March but didn't go to my first meeting until September. At first I was nervous but I soon felt comfortable and that I belonged there.

Before I joined NAAFA I never thought a guy would like me *because* of my weight—I thought maybe someone might like me *despite* my weight. When men would say, "I love your legs," or "your body," I'd say to myself, "Oh, this is a sick number—it's like digging someone with no arms or who's maimed." After four years in therapy I got to the point where I thought maybe someone could like Gloria Cohen. In NAAFA some of us find that being fat is only one thing we are and we shouldn't let everything be colored by that.

In my opinion, fat admirers have a lot more problems

than fat women. A lot of them are in the closet about what they like. They'll have "at-home" relationships and say they love you but they won't go out of the house with you. I feel if I'm good enough for someone to go to bed with me I should be good enough for them to take me out. So I date less than some of the other NAAFA ladies. Some of the women would rather have an at-home relationship than nothing at all. And why shouldn't they have sex? They're horny like everyone else. Even if a man can't handle going out in public with them, most of the women can sympathize.

Doreen Katz is another member of the New York chapter of NAAFA who talked about some common difficulties of fat women. She is twenty-six years old and weighs about 250 pounds. Doreen is unemployed and lives with her parents and sisters.

Doreen Katz

My whole family is overweight. Everyone hates it and hates to diet. My mother is miserable being fat and she tells me how I've missed out on life being fat. My mother thinks all my problems are due to my weight— that if I lost weight I'd get married and have a great job.

Even this afternoon I was sitting and watching television, and my mother said to me, "Boy, you're fat."

My sister just got engaged, and my mother said "We can't all be fat at the wedding; it would look horrible. Someone has to diet."

My sister is heavy and her boyfriend is thin. My mother keeps wondering why he would pick my sister when he could get a thin girl.

I've had a lot of bad experiences with diet doctors, and doctors in general. A fat person hates to go to the doctor. Even if you go to the doctor because of a cold, the doctor will say "lose fifty pounds" as if that will take care of the cold. I belonged to HIP (a prepaid health plan) and was assigned to a doctor. I had a cold, walked into his office and he looked at me and said, "I'm not going to treat you unless you lose weight." I said, "I just want some cough medicine so I won't cough myself to death." He said, "Okay. I'll give you some cough medicine, but if you don't lose twenty pounds in two weeks, don't come back."

I was also assigned to a woman gynecologist who told me she didn't want to treat me unless I lost weight. I went to have my birth control pills extended, and she said, "I can't give you the pill because you have high blood pressure." I said, "How do you know, you haven't taken it." She said, "You're fat—you have high blood pressure." But then she agreed to give me the pill if I didn't have high blood pressure. A heavy nurse took it, and it was normal. The doctor was shocked, and she just gave me two months' worth of a prescription, even though most doctors will give you pills for a year.

I've tried all kinds of ways to lose weight. I was interested in having intestinal bypass surgery, but it's dangerous and expensive. Insurance won't pay for it, and doctors are charging over two thousand dollars for the surgical fee alone. One doctor told me if I had it he would take out my gall bladder or appendix so my insurance would at least pay for the hospital bill, but I'd have to pay his fee for the surgery.

I also tried to get into a six-month residential program that uses the liquid protein diet at the Rockefeller Institute, but I couldn't get in because you have to be self-supporting so you can work in the hospital.

I go to a pill-pusher doctor now who has a whole string of offices all over the city. You sit there waiting for hours for each visit—even though you have an appointment. You just go there and check in and then you can check out to go to the movies or something until it's your turn. These places are packed and the nurse actually sits there selling rings and jewelry to the patients. She has a jewelry concession right in the office. They never take your blood pressure or anything. They just look at your card and give you pills. One doctor asked me just one question. He wanted to know whether I was a bookkeeper. I told him no and asked him what did that have to do with it. He said bookkeepers never lose weight.

When I was younger I flirted with men a lot. When I

was a teenager being big made me look older—when I was fifteen I looked twenty. So older guys were interested in me and I got into a lot of trouble because I was really too young for them.

Now I find that I have to settle more than I used to—I have to take my pick out of what's available. I can't really flirt with any men I want to, especially since I have such a fear of rejection.

I've asked the men I meet at NAAFA why they like heavy women. One said "My mother was heavy and I loved her—she was so soft and warm." They like the way the fat feels. They like being enveloped in it. They like the pressure of the weight. They don't want you to wear a bra or girdle—they want the fat to wiggle. I don't like it when men like me just because I'm fat—I'm like an object then, although I know most men pick women initially on the basis of their looks.

A lot of men go out with fat women because they're easy, they're grateful for the attention. The men figure you're starved for attention and food, so if they feed you, sex can't be far behind. And they think if you're fat you have oral fixations and you'll like oral sex.

It's hard for them, too. They get asked, "How could you go out with her? She's so fat." Or, "Couldn't you get better than that?" They know what they like, but there's also what society dictates.

There are many common themes in the life experiences of NAAFA women. Before joining the organization several lived isolated lives. Many had few friends and either lived with their parents or had close human contact only with siblings and parents. But even these relationships were seldom gratifying since their weight was often the focus of family strains and fights.

After joining NAAFA many were gradually drawn into a social world of peers where they felt unjudged, among comrades. For many, joining NAAFA was the beginning not only of friendships, greater self-confidence, and being able to leave their apartments, but also of dating and sexual relationships.

But with the exception of Rhetta Moskowitz and a few women who have found long-term partners in NAAFA, few of the single women seem really satisfied with the relationships they have made with men through NAAFA. Joan Fralley, a thirty-five-year-old secretary, echoes the words of many others in the organization when she explains that the most rewarding relationships she has formed in NAAFA are friendships with other women.

Joan Fralley

Many women in NAAFA are promiscuous in their search for love and acceptance. I find the dances boring and beneath me. Ten years ago I would have been there looking for someone; ten years ago I would have been promiscuous myself. But I think without love, sex is nothing. Some of the women think they're going to find someone wonderful and they see someone passable and then project all their fantasies and paste their desires onto that person. At the last dance, Judy, who is twenty-two years old, told me she was in love with a man who was there. She had never seen him before, and he was very good looking. It turned out that he left the dance with another woman. Judy never actually talked with him but she fell in love and was crushed when she didn't meet him.

Personally, I think a man who would go to a dance looking only for a fat woman is deranged. I only want to have something to do with a man who likes me regardless of my size.

Some of these men are very compulsive about having sex right away and with someone new every week. In a way they have something in common with the women in NAAFA. Some of us have to have food immediately and when we're binging nothing else matters—we must have our food. Some of the fat admirers are like this about sex with women. But they don't have a straightforward attraction to fat women. It's distorted in some way. And they often criticize what they profess to like. When they meet a new man at a dance many NAAFA women feel that for the first time they've found the man of their dreams. It's so unrealistic. And they will allow an awful lot—they take a lot of shit. Being walked on and disappointed. It's only when the guy comes right out and tells them he's more attracted to some other woman that they see how unrealistic they've been, and then they're crumpled.

Some of the fat admirers and the NAAFA women make psychological deals: "Don't mention I'm fat and ugly and I won't mention that you're small or bald or you have no personality." These men want unconditional love. Some NAAFA women marry black men who want a white woman and look at the NAAFA women as damaged white women. After they get married they start criticizing the women about their weight. Then there are fat admirers who are nice but many of them have no backbone. They're led around by whatever woman they're with. I think the feelings involved have to do with being a baby.

The men who are sexually aggressive also like the fat in an infantile way—they like to pump and knead the breasts, like a kitten nursing.

So I would say there are three kinds of men who are attracted only to fat women: the *nursers* who are infantile, the *dealers* who exchange not acknowledging the fat if the woman will accept their faults unconditionally, and the *users* who want a lay and know fat women are vulnerable and will put up with anything.

In a way, all of us make deals. But the thing that is most damaging for fat women is when we lie to ourselves.

Fat admirers may not seem like very appealing or sympathetic characters in some of these descriptions, but it is important to consider things from their perspective as well. Many fat admirers in NAAFA talk about how confused and deeply ashamed they were about their sexual inclinations: how freakish they felt about being sexually unresponsive toward slender women whom everyone else considers the ideal sex object. It has also been difficult for them to acknowledge to themselves and others that they are attracted to fat women. As one fat admirer explained, it had taken repeated humiliating experiences to learn that he was simply unable to have an erection with an average-sized woman.

Conventional attitudes do indeed regard the tastes of fat admirers as perverted or at least as symptomatic of neurosis.

In cartoons and other popular media, the small man who is married to a large woman is typically depicted as being enslaved by a bossy, domineering, asexual woman. Moreover, that a man would *seek out* such a woman, rather than merely tolerate someone who became fat after he married her, is particularly interpreted as the manifestation of some sort of mother fixation and either infantile or incestuous inclinations.

During a discussion about the problems of fat people and fat admirers at a recent convention of NAAFA, the conversation focused on the strains between the men and women in the organization. One of the smaller women (about 220 pounds) opened the conversation by pointing out that women of her size had more trouble attracting men than NAAFA's larger women. She was too large for conventional men and too small for NAAFA men. Another woman explained how hurt she was by her current boyfriend who insisted they come to conventions separately so he would have the opportunity to meet other fat women.

Still another was upset by a man who had claimed to love her but who lost interest when she lost weight: "I'm the same person. How does a woman deal with someone who's turned on only by fat?"

In reply, a fat admirer countered that ten times as many men would fall out of love with a woman if she *gained* weight and this would be viewed as understandable. So, he asked, were fat admirers really so different from other men in being attracted to a specific body configuration?

Another fat admirer echoed this defense: "Sexual attraction is instinctual, not political. We can't help it when we're turned off when a woman loses weight. You can't have your cake and eat it too."

The first man recounted that when he was young he liked a fat girl he was dating but because his preference embarrassed him he couldn't bring himself to tell her that he *liked* her fat. When she lost weight, thinking it would please him, he found it devastating.

A woman replied that some of the women in NAAFA had been warned by their doctors that they needed to lose weight, and they were distressed to know that if they lost weight to avoid illness, they would also lose their boyfriends.

Still another woman argued that it *was* a political issue and that women didn't have such specific physical requirements for men as men had for them. When one of the fat admirers asked her if *she* didn't really have physical preferences in men, she replied, "I don't have any choice—I have to take what I can get. For many fat admirers, women are interchangeable. Our minds aren't important to you."

Finally, one of the men repeated again that while he couldn't deny that he was attracted by a specific body type, so were so-called normal men: "I actually have less specific physical criteria than most men. I'm attracted to women who weigh 170 or 270 or 370. Most men are only attracted to women who weigh between 100 and 135. So who's got more of a fetish?"

The issues and questions raised by NAAFA are important and illuminating. NAAFA offers a perspective on the problems of fat people and what to do about them that is regrettably missing from most concepts of obesity. By stressing how fat people suffer most of all from exclusion, discrimination, ridicule and consequent self-hatred, NAAFA calls attention to the political and social as well as the individual causes and nature of their problems.

Dieting is not the simple solution to fat people's problems. By stressing this, NAAFA introduces a more sophisticated analysis of the situation. As NAAFA members know well, fat people are statistically unlikely to become thin and stay that way. By emphasizing self-acceptance and consciousness-raising rather than diet, NAAFA advocates a more realistic and much less oppressive solution. NAAFA members discover that current conventional ideas of beauty are not universal and have an opportunity to see themselves as attractive people capable of loving and being loved.

NAAFA is politically oriented, but it is not closed to psychological introspection. Most of its members are thoughtful and honest enough with themselves to face the painful personal components of their situation. By and large the women who belong to NAAFA are neither radicals nor feminists. Most have traditional values and ideas concerning love and marriage. They don't want to change sex roles or the structure of relationships between American men and women. They merely want to be able to participate. As the women quoted earlier admit, even though it is unjust and arbitrary, being fat in this society has certain consequences, and for single women, one of the consequences is that the pool of available men is severely restricted.

Finally, what is most interesting about NAAFA is that it shows people resisting discouraging forces to gain self-respect and to demand respect from others. While its members do not deny their unhappiness or vulnerabilities, they attempt to use their strengths to achieve satisfying lives. That fat people, so often pushed in isolation, passivity, self-loathing, and despair, should organize and struggle is a heartening and impressive thing.

2

Overeaters Anonymous: A Program of Recovery

My daughter was going to spend Christmas with her grandmother and she baked some cookies to bring along. I'm jealous of my daughter because she's a beautiful nine-year-old who has her whole life ahead of her. While she was at school I ate all the cookies she baked for her grandmother.

There was no way I could replace them for her. They were love. She and my husband couldn't believe that I ate those cookies. My husband asked me how I could do it.

—*Laura R.*,
a speaker at a meeting
of Overeaters Anonymous

Overeaters Anonymous describes itself as a program of recovery for people who are compulsive overeaters. Modeled closely upon Alcoholics Anonymous, it regards overeating as a compulsive disease that is serious, self-destructive and capable of ruining a person's life. Like alcoholism, compulsive overeating is viewed as the manifestation of a progressive physical, psychological, and spiritual disease that is never cured but may be "arrested" through strict adherence to the program. OA was started in 1960 by a woman known as Roxanne S., who thought her compulsive eating was a disease similar to alcoholism. The organization now has thousands of chapters that meet weekly all across the United States. It is nonprofit and completely supported by small contributions from its members, mostly women.

Overeaters Anonymous is a very significant organization because it expresses an increasingly popular view: that obesity indicates deep psychological disturbances, that its cause and cure rest with the individual. The assumption that the fat person is creating her own misery and that she can stop doing it is, of course, basic to all treatments for fat people, whether they stress changing eating habits (as do Weight Watchers, children's diet camps, or behavior modification) or working out underlying emotional problems (as in psychotherapy). A look at Overeaters Anonymous is particularly illuminating because OA carries the gospel of personal change to its extreme: it offers its members nothing less than a spiritual and physical rebirth. And because members look deeply within themselves to find the causes of their suffering, a look at the organization also offers insight into some of the psychological dynamics of being fat.

When OA members talk about not being in control, they mean more than not being able to control what they eat: each member typically comes to see that she has mistaken views about what she, as an individual, can or cannot control in life and in the world. OA therefore gives its members more than a method for "abstinence" from overeating: it provides them with a set of principles to guide them through such existential waters as guilt, loss, personal responsibility, and acceptance.

The first and constantly repeated thing that members must do is acknowledge to themselves and the group that they are compulsive overeaters, powerless when faced with food. Instead of blaming outside forces for their problems they are made to recognize that their suffering and shame have been created by their own compulsive overeating.

Karen: I lost 35 pounds and now I've put on 40 because I said, "Why me?" instead of saying, "I'm a compulsive overeater."

Joe: I'm a compulsive drug addict, gambler, alcoholic, overeater. Why me? Because I did it to myself. No one else.

Laura: At one time I was eating myself to death. I've
learned that overeating is a death wish, suicide.

Joanie: Most of us are victims of an emotional illness. Most
of us have a tendency toward depression. Society puts the
hangups on us and a lot of what we're blamed for isn't
our fault, but it is in a way. Because we allow people to
hurt us. People will treat us as we treat ourselves. If we
treat ourselves like crap so will others.

The meetings usually take place in a simple room (often at
a church, library or some other community building. Sitting
in a circle the members open the meeting by chanting, in
unison, their Prayer of Serenity. There are other ritual prelimi-
naries: a reading of the Steps and Traditions of the organization
and selections from OA and AA literature. The leader for the
day introduces herself by saying (as all members must do before
speaking), "Hi. My name is [first name] and I'm a compulsive
overeater." the other group members then answer in unison,
"Hi——. Welcome."

During a meeting, several give their pitch, telling what their
lives were like before joining OA, what happened to them in
the organization, and what their lives are like now. Each statement is typically applauded by the other members, and, indeed,
all contributions are applauded and applauded alike. At the
end, the members stand and join hands in a circle, chanting
in unison the Lord's Prayer and the OA slogan, "Keep coming
back."

There are special chapters for teenage compulsive overeaters, couples, and gay members, and there are "O-Anon" chapters to help family members and friends of compulsive overeaters. There are also annual national and regional conventions,
attended by thousands of members who stay up late into the
nights to participate in marathon sessions and study groups.

Undoubtedly most people first come to OA because they
want to lose weight, and not because they are seeking a new
way of life. Most have tried other weight-reducing methods
and initially view OA as only one more. And, as one member
put it, it is one of the few programs that "doesn't cost an arm
and a leg." But no matter what brings them initially, those who
remain in Overeaters Anonymous come to define their weight
problem as merely the external symptom of deeper troubles.

As members frequently remark, they "come for the diet and stay for the program."

Indeed, the concept of dieting is soon replaced with the more meaning-laden notion of "abstaining," one day at a time, from compulsive overeating. Abstinence is defined as adhering to a prearranged eating plan that allows only "three weighed and measured meals a day with nothing in between." A new member, sometimes called a "baby," is asked to write down her daily eating plan and report it by telephone every morning to her group sponsor. She is not allowed to depart from the plan in even the slightest way without first talking about it with the sponsor, who will try to dissuade her. The OA-recommended diet is practically devoid of carbohydrates, because it is believed in OA that many people are "carbohydrate sensitive," and that eating any carbohydrates at all will make them crave more and more.

For OA, abstinence has a sacred or magical quality. "Abstinence is without exception the most important thing in our lives" is a constant refrain. Members count to the day and constantly report the length of time they have "kept abstinence," even after years. Although the member is asked only to abstain day by day, there is always the threat that if she departs from the eating plan in even the slightest way, she will lose everything. Like the alcoholic who may fall off the wagon with one drink, so is the OA member taught that she is only a bite away from a binge and personal disaster.

Such long and extraordinary records of "perfectly maintained back to back" abstinence are routinely reported that it is hard not to wonder whether the letter of the law isn't sometimes substituted for the spirit in order to maintain a perfect record. This seemed to be the case during a northeastern regional convention held at the Concord Hotel in the Catskill Mountains of New York. Ironically, the Concord, a Jewish Borscht-Belt hotel, serves unremittingly huge portions of food to its guests. But during the OA convention it was presumably serving only meals consistent with the OA Grey Sheet diet.

One evening the hotel was offering roast chicken for dinner. The OA eating plan allows for "two pieces" of chicken, but the hotel was serving portions consisting of half chickens (and large ones at that) to each diner. Since each piece was half a chicken, common sense should have dictated that one piece certainly used up the allowance of the diet, but one member explained to the waiter that she was entitled to two. When the waiter returned with a complete extra serving (including more vegetables) and told her she could take the whole thing, the diner indignantly rejected the second helping of vegetables and protested to her fellow members at the table (who remained silent) that she only wanted the second piece of chicken that was "coming to her" according to the OA eating plan.

Whether or not members eat more than the program allows, the incident broadly illustrates the very orthodox view OA and its members hold about the rules and traditions. Not only are these principles scrupulously upheld, but they are repeated over and over again at meetings, like a litany. Considering, also, the enormous amount of time that members give to the organization (meetings several times a week, daily phone calls) one might well ask whether the program isn't just exchanging different forms of compulsive behavior. This was jokingly implied by one member (a slim young woman) during a regional convention session entitled "Substituting One Compulsion For Another":

> I was sitting at a table and a very handsome man asked if he could join me. I said all right. He ordered a drink and asked if I wanted one. I said I didn't drink. He asked if I wanted to have dinner and I told him I didn't eat that kind of food. He asked if I would go home with him and I told him no. He said to me, "You don't drink, you don't eat, you don't have sex. What do you do?" I said "I have three measured meals a day with nothing in between."

Apart from abstinence, nothing is treated more reverently in OA than The Twelve Steps toward recovery, each one being undertaken with the help of a sponsor and with reading and writing assignments:

1. We admitted we were powerless over food—that our lives had become unmanageable.

2. Came to believe that a Power greater than ourselves could restore us to sanity.

3. Made a decision to turn our will and our lives over to the care of God as we understood Him.

4. Made a searching and fearless moral inventory of ourselves.

5. Admitted to God, to ourselves and to another human being the exact nature of our wrongs.

6. Were entirely ready to have God remove all these defects of character.

7. Humbly asked Him to remove our shortcomings.

8. Made a list of all persons we had harmed, and became willing to make amends to them all.

9. Made direct amends to such people wherever possible, except when to do so would injure them or others.

10. Continued to take personal inventory and when we were wrong, promptly admitted it.

11. Sought through prayer and meditation to improve our conscious contact with God as we understood Him, praying only for knowledge of His will for us and the power to carry that out.

12. Having had a spiritual awakening as the result of these steps, we tried to carry this message to compulsive overeaters and practice these principles in all our affairs.

God is everywhere in this, but *God* is ambiguous. OA repeatedly points out that the Higher Power is only what each member understands Him to be. In the member's mind, God can be a conventional spiritual figure or the OA organization or local group. What is important is that the member surrenders her "will" to a force beyond or larger than herself and acknowledges that she is not in control.

This is a key point. OA philosophy and the personal stories told there revolve around the idea that the fat person has a confused and erroneous relationship to personal control. She is either not in control where she could be (for example, her eating), self-deluded in believing that she has control where she doesn't (for example, in thinking she is responsible for tragic events in life, or that she doesn't need the help of a higher power). The latter leads to unrealistic "pride" ("I needed to lose not only weight but my size 44 ego" is often heard) and to unnecessary guilt for tragic events or mistaken confi-

dence in her ability to lick her problems by herself. The Serenity
Prayer, recited at every meeting, reminds the member of her
need to better distinguish what she can and can't control:

> God grant me the Serenity to accept the things I cannot
> change, the Courage to change the things I can, and the
> Wisdom to know the difference.

In keeping with this principle, the member is repeatedly
urged not to blame herself for her failures and imperfections,
for no one is perfect (except God): "Sometimes when we think
we have failed we will remember we are not failures and when
we make mistakes we will remember we are not mistakes,"
is a phrase that is often quoted at OA. The individual suffers
from guilt, OA says, in order to preserve two mistaken ideas:
that she is capable of being perfect, and that she is in control.
To believe that one is responsible for external events may give
the individual a false sense of pride and specialness, but it will
exact a heavy price in guilt. Instead, teaches OA, the member
should learn that she can control certain things (like what goes
into her mouth) but the rest must be "turned over" to a Higher
Power. Reminding oneself of these limitations is one of the
constant themes of the stories told in OA:

Marion: I have been obese all of my life. I managed to
maintain my weight in the 190s for eleven years but now
I've had six months of abstinence. I wasn't happy—I
used to blame it on my weight. I knew there was a
growing distance in my marriage. I kept trying to change
it, not knowing I had to accept the things I cannot
change. One month after the OA convention last year I
told my husband to get out of my life. He was
homosexual . . . I also tried to be a perfect daughter—
except that I was obese. Many of us are people pleasers,
but I am in love with *me* now. I'll be thirty in two
months. My thirties will be for me. God grant me the
Serenity to accept the things I cannot change, the
Courage to change the things I can, and the Wisdom to
know the difference. [She cries.]

Barbara: I was married three times, and I have become a
widow three times. I was separated from loved ones by

an act of God, and I am not God, and I didn't kill anybody.

Similarly, OA teaches that although it is painful to give up the hopes of the past, the member will gain the benefits of the present only by making that renunciation. Like refusing to acknowledge that one is not in control of life, holding on to the past brings some comfort but much more pain. In a convention session devoted to the question "Can I Get Back Those Lost Years?" participants spoke to the issue:

Jane: My name is Jane and I'm a fat, compulsive overeater. Last year I was five sizes smaller. I used to live in a world of "if only" and "what if." "If only I had taken my mother to the doctor in time she would still be alive." "If only I married someone else." "If only I was sixteen and knew what I know now." I lived not for today but for yesterday or tomorrow. I've learned in OA that life is constantly changing. Don't stay with something but change. If you're in a bad marriage or a bad job, get out. . . .

Debbie: Growing up fat is not easy. I went through life not experiencing anything. Any club that would have me as a member, I didn't want. I missed out. My top weight was 240 pounds. I was surrounding myself in a wall of fat. I've been married for sixteen years but not happily. There were days when I didn't get dressed or talk to anyone. Someone dragged me to OA, and I got the body of a sixteen-year-old that I didn't have when I was sixteen. A few months ago I developed a mad, wild crush on a boy of sixteen I work with. I'm thirty-four. I didn't understand it. I talked to no one about it—I was ashamed. The first mistake I made was that the first person I told was the boy. That didn't work out. I told my husband, and he was understanding [she laughs]. I talked to OA people and learned that I wasn't alone. It happens to people who lose weight and want to get back the lost years. I realized that the problem wasn't that the boy wasn't interested in me or that I had a husband but the problem was within me. I was rejecting who I was now to be fifteen. So I had to apply my new wisdom to who I was now, not who I was at fifteen. We can't go back and I can't undo something I did before. I accept that I flubbed it and I can't undo it.

The same theme of giving up the disappointed hopes of the past was reiterated in a convention session entitled "Strength Is Not Holding On But Letting Go":

Carolyn: When I came into this program four years ago I was a wreck. Physically I was 187 pounds. Mentally I was miserable. Spiritually I was nowhere. I was going through all kinds of problems. My son was not doing well and I was holding on to everything and I slowly learned to use the Serenity Prayer. Then I moved to Florida and had a new set of problems including my marriage which was an old problem I brought with me.

When I talked about them with my husband before, I would always panic and say, "No—you can't leave me. I can't make it alone." I was desperate at the thought of our marriage ending. I was finally completing the fourth step. [Made a searching and fearless inventory of ourselves.] And I was talking to my sponsor about my fear of letting go. As a child I was always afraid of being left alone. I took this fear along with me into adult life. As I related this to my sponsor it occurred to me that it was the same thing I felt toward my husband—but now I'm a grown woman, not a child. So I was able to start to let go of my husband. I decided I could tell him it's okay if we separate. I have just begun a new life. I am free of an unhappy, destructive marriage. I am not alone because of OA. In that letting go I found strength.

Most of these themes are ultimately related to the member's presumed central problem of confusion over personal control, but OA offers wisdom and guidance as well on the emotional experiences of guilt, loss, and giving up the past. One could say that Overeaters Anonymous attempts mass psychotherapy, for these are universal themes and insights that, in our culture, people frequently discover in therapy. OA's pronouncements concerning these subjects are stated generally enough so that they can be applied to a wide variety of cases by individual members. Still, when OA wisdoms are repeated like a litany it is natural to wonder how deeply the message has been absorbed. In the convention session devoted to "Strength Is Not Holding On But Letting Go," mentioned earlier, one speaker strung together a wide assortment of OA aphorisms, but hit an unconvincing note:

Ellen: I'm hurting. I was rejected about an hour ago. It was an old tape—a 262-pound tape. I'm supposed to say "rejection is another man's preference." I'm letting go of the rejection. Without my abstinence I have no life. Don't compare, just relate, because comparing can lead to tearing. I've let go of a lot of things.

It is hard to know how effective the program really is. Since last names are not used and members do not get weighed or report weights in any systematic manner, there is no way to evaluate the organization's success with long-term weight control. But often those who stay feel their eating has come under control and also feel they have undergone a profound personal transformation. Of course, this impression is partly fostered by the organization's instructions to members to talk of how their lives have changed since joining OA. As in AA meetings, there are frequent descriptions of how the member's former compulsiveness had led her to "hit rock bottom." For example, many talk of how they used to stay in bed all day and get up only to eat and go to the bathroom. No matter how sad, the autobiographies always end on a note of hopefulness and gratitude:

Fred: Last year I was dead and today I am living.

Ellen: I met my present husband when I was 30 pounds more than now.... We have a pretty good sex life but the weight was a problem. Under the sheets I was huffing and puffing, and I thought, "If this isn't over soon I'll get a stroke." I liked a water bed because it was no effort—I'd lay still so the fat would be smooth. Darkness was my friend. As the fat came off I was able to move sexually. Now I'm not ashamed and I don't want to hide. Being heavy is a repression of everything. When I was fat, I had to make love for acceptance. Now I can say no—and I can also be the aggressor. And now I'm not afraid of the lights.

The feeling of hope and recovery from a life that had become "unmanageable" is also nicely illustrated by a speaker who led a convention session entitled "Accepting The Things I Cannot Change":

Annie: I don't know when the first awareness hit me that I was chubby and different from other children. When I was three and a half my mother took me somewhere without a bathing suit and she wanted me to swim in my underpants, and even at three and a half I resisted physical exposure. I recall being called "Hey, fat" "Hey, blimp" "Hey, you with the headlight". I was the only child in nursery school who was not allowed chocolate milk at lunch time. In the first grade we put on a play about an Eskimo who was supposed to get stuck in the door to the igloo, and I was chosen for the part. . . . My life was of total degradation and humiliation. Gym classes were horrible. Even though I was athletic I could never climb ropes. I had to be in the base of the pyramid in tumbling. . . . When I was in the fifth grade we were weighed in gym class in alphabetical order. I was an *R,* so I was near the end of the line, but there were still several people behind me, and when it was my turn they all crowded behind to find out how much I weighed. Then someone screamed there was a man in the girl's locker room and everyone rushed in and it turned out it was just men's shoes someone had seen. But they were my corrective shoes. I had to tell everyone. I went from one degradation to another.
. . . My parents always interrogated me: "What's in your mouth? What are you chewing? What are you doing in the kitchen? In your friend's house?" It got so eating in front of them was unpleasant. Eating anywhere else was illicit.
. . . At age 12 the diet pills and shots began. . . . I tried the vibrator, electrodes, Ayds, Stillman, hypnosis . . . , psychoanalysis. No one ever told me I had a compulsive disease.

. . . I got slim at age eighteen and met my husband. At the time I met him I wore a size 16. When we were engaged I wore an 18, and a 20-plus by the time we got married. I say 20 plus because at the initial fitting for the wedding I wore a 20. On the last fitting the dress wouldn't close by four inches so they had to destroy another dress and take off sashes to cover the gap. We paid for one and a half dresses. My mother sewed me into the dress for the wedding, but my husband had to get me out of it.

. . . In June 1975 when I was thirty-four, I became an invalid. I was well over 100 pounds overweight. My youth had always helped me allay the physical stress. In 1975 I began to experience crippling chest pains—like a heart attack. All the cardiograms denied heart involvement, but I could no longer walk half a block without crippling pains. The doctor had immediately put me on a diet, but the pains grew worse. One day I had an attack when I was in the supermarket, and I was rushed to the cardiac unit. For several weeks I was the recipient of every test.

. . . I hoped they would find the reason for my overweight. . . . The tests showed I had a moderate hiatus hernia that didn't cause the attacks. My blood pressure was very high, but my blood chemistry was normal. The diagnosis was "obese female . . . chest pain . . . cause unknown". The doctor said I fell into a small group who experienced angina without a reason. He said I would just have to learn to live with pain—as an invalid.

Time and my weight progressed. A friend asked me to join OA. I thought if I didn't have to walk up stairs I could make it.

The OA group I joined . . . allowed only the Grey Sheet [diet]. . . . I almost walked out. But there were three beautiful women when I was about to go who cornered me and pleaded with me to stay.

If these three people loved me so instantly, how could I say, "Bug off?" OA may have helped me rewrite medical history. After one week of negative carbohydrates my pains disappeared. Now I can walk, run, and ride a bicycle. I had an allergy to carbohydrates— they were poison to me.

OA has taught me honesty. I have been my own victim. Today I accept the things I cannot change, I change what I can, and with serenity I turn the rest over to God.

In most respects, Overeaters Anonymous represents a perspective on the suffering of fat people that is directly opposed to that offered by NAAFA, yet both reveal what it's like to be fat. If NAAFA illuminates some of the social and political reasons why fat people suffer, then OA delves into some of the psychological syndromes that many overweight individuals experience, particularly paradoxical feelings about personal control that are unrealistically excessive in some ways and markedly diminished in others. If NAAFA tries to convince fat people not to pin their hopes on a great transformation when they lose weight, then OA members certainly choose the opposite strategy. But despite these differences, there are also many common features in the organizations that highlight some aspects of being fat.

One of NAAFA's major arguments is that a person should not have to be thin to deserve the full roster of human rights and privileges, and that self-acceptance and acceptance by others should not be conditional on a person's weight. It would seem that NAAFA recognizes that unconditional acceptance is somehow necessary for people who have been told all their lives that losing weight is the necessary condition of being included in the human race.

While NAAFA demands full acceptance for its members in the outside world, OA offers unconditional acceptance in a different way. One of the informal rules of OA is that its members should not judge each other or "take inventory" of anyone else. In fact, OA draws distinctions between members as little as possible, and stresses universal problems. Differences are minimized or avoided: members learn not to argue or disagree with one another. As one convention speaker put it, "Where else can someone look at two hundred or three hundred people they've never seen before and know there is not one stranger in the room?" No "leaders" are allowed to dominate the organization, and it is felt that everyone has something to offer—a message. "With OA you never have to be alone again, and whether you like someone or not, if you say you need help they will help you," is the way one member described unconditional acceptance.

Overeaters Anonymous pursues unconditional acceptance in another sense. Even though many members have been failures in the eyes of the outside world, it is impossible to fail as an OA member. As long as a member "keeps coming back" she is treated as a success. Members are applauded for keeping their abstinence, and they are applauded for wanting to try again if they lose it. In OA, as long as a member returns, she has fulfilled the only requirement for complete acceptance.

OA and NAAFA also share the assumption that fat people tend to live isolated lives and may even need to be resocialized in order to rejoin society:

Francine: After my husband left me I was glad to be left alone without anyone picking on me, and glad to have my refrigerator. But inside I was really dead. I'm glad I have OA now.

Pat: When I came into OA a year ago I walked in a twenty-nine-year-old with the maturity of a teenager. I was afraid of relationships; I had never learned that relationships are based on mutuality.

But while NAAFA explains isolation as the product of social exclusion, OA argues that solitariness and furtiveness stem from the member's compulsion to overeat:

Annie: For the compulsive eater the urge to eat takes precedence over his family, work, social life and is without regard for consequential physical, mental, or emotional impairment.

Betty: When I was in the eighth grade at 190 pounds, I would tell my mother every night that I was going to the library. I would steal a five-dollar bill from my mother's drawer every evening and go to the delicatessen next door and buy food and then sit in the back of the library and eat it. I can't believe I did something like that to my own mother.

John: I used to play hooky from school so I could stay home and eat. I'd pretend to be sick so my parents would

let me stay home. When I was twelve or thirteen my
parents had a 25th anniversary party and I brought home
half of a huge cake from the party. I was supposed to be
on a diet, but I played sick and stayed home from school.
At first I was cutting the cake from an angle to disguise
that I was eating it. But then I kept eating. When there
was only a little left I purposely dropped it on the floor,
picked it up and ate it. Then I gave one crumb to the
dog. Then I called up my mother at work and told her
that while I was trying to get a glass of milk from the
refrigerator I knocked the cake on the floor and so I gave
it to the dog.

There is particular emphasis placed in OA on the importance
of making sure a member is not left alone. Over and over the
member is reminded that she is just a telephone call away from
the help of a sponsor, and OA members (like members of
NAAFA) apparently do spend considerable time on the telephone. In most large cities, the OA member can find a meeting
on any day or night of the week. At holiday times that are
especially difficult for maintaining abstinence (such as Thanks-
giving and Christmas) the organization offers twenty-four-hour
marathon meetings, as it does at the regional conventions.

Quite simply, the OA member is assured that no matter
what terrible things may happen in her life, she need never be
alone.

Jennifer: I am divorced—I have been for four years. I have
    a child who is four and a half years old, and I am a full-
    time student. My marriage was very painful, and the best
    thing I ever did was get a divorce. It took adjustment to
    being single. I didn't want to be hurt anymore. I
    withdrew. Built up walls. Put myself in total isolation
    and kept eating. I tried Weight Watchers, amphetamines,
    behavior modification. I returned to OA a year ago. I had
    a need for friendship, love and sharing. I found this in
    OA. We as single people have special needs. We do not
    have a support system. We need OA more than others.
    OA helped me not only to change my eating problem but
    gave me different ways to solve my problems besides
    shoving food in my mouth. I still have a lot of
    problems—in fact I'm just breaking up with someone

I've been going with for a year and a half. He's
wonderful . . . but we're not right for each other. I feel
depression and loneliness. I worry about my daughter. I
have no one to share things with. I don't want to be
alone. I need OA.

Finally, OA, like NAAFA, raises questions about the relationship between the problems of fat women and the problems
of other women in this society. Although OA defines its membership only in terms of compulsive overeating, in fact, most
of its members (it would seem well over 90 percent) are
women. And although members believe that the cause of their
suffering rests in themselves, many of the problems they talk
about are found among all women in the society: subordination
in their relationships with men, coping with the problems of
divorce and the feelings of loneliness and failure divorce in-
spires:

Caroline: I too had a marriage that was unhappy, and I hung
   on like a bulldog. When my marriage failed and my
   husband said he didn't love me anymore I thought I had
   failed at the one thing I knew how to do—please a man.
   Not how to be an adult woman. Now I am learning to be
   the person God meant me to be.

Doreen: I've been married twice and had a lover once. The
   first time I married a man fourteen years older. I was
   eighteen and married to get out of the house. My father
   was not an affectionate man, and I looked for someone to
   give me what my father hadn't. I had a beautiful son and
   threw my husband out. He was looking for a mother and
   I was looking for a father. He couldn't accept a child. I
   was single again. I needed a job, but I was fat, so I lost
   weight and got a job at, you should pardon the
   expression, a pizza parlor.
   I met a man who was a widower with two children—I
   met him in December and married him in April. Once
   again, he was older and I was looking for a replacement
   for my father. As it turned out, he was brutal and I was
   often beaten up. One day I took a knife to him and said,
   "just try it one more time." I became single again and I
   decided I would never get married. For the second time I

returned to my mother's house—I was once again a child with her own child. I finally got an apartment of my own, got a job working nights and met a nice man. He was married and had four children but I loved him and he loved me. His wife was a good wife and mother so he couldn't leave her. He and I had a ball because he had no responsibility to me. We ate, drank, gambled, sneaked around. Last year my friend had a stroke, and he's paralyzed on the right side and can't speak too well. So once again I became single again. I had to get around hospital visiting hours not to see his family. I became sober—dry. Food I was still eating. He got some rehabilitation, and by this time I was in the OA program. I said to him, "do you want to come home with me?" because I felt I owed him something, but he said no, as I hoped he would. If he had come home with me I would have had to give up this program because I go to six or seven meetings a week.

Single is being alone. Having nobody else. I was in depression and self-pity many times. Last March 15 I was going to commit suicide. I arranged for my son to live with a cousin and saw that my mother was settled in Florida. When I came back I was going to commit suicide with pills and booze. This program saved my life. I had heard of OA from my psychiatrist a few months before.

In OA I learned something about myself. I *am* lonely. But that's OK for today. Through the program I learned that "never" and "can't" are no such things. I am single—but I am not lonely. I have the program and friends. I didn't have friends for many years before I joined this program. I have God—not of a religion. He is only how I choose to see him.

One could argue that being fat is the least of the troubles OA members face. But for many, being fat comes to symbolize what is wrong in their lives and controlling their eating habits represents a sense of personal efficacy. If life doesn't offer many opportunities to feel potent, it may be comforting to focus one's attentions on the few activities one can control.

Most of the members of OA are from working-class backgrounds. Few can afford intensive or long-term psychotherapy, and few seem to be involved in women's consciousness-raising or support groups. Without OA, many would indeed be isolated. Although OA is fundamentally apolitical in its perspective, in fact it reassures and brings together women who have failed in society's eyes as women: whether because they are fat or poor or divorced or single or have problems with their children.

In many ways, OA, like NAAFA, rescues people from social isolation and makes their most shameful feature precisely the cause around which they may rally and find comrades and approval. NAAFA asks its members to stop hiding their bodies and to walk in the world with pride. OA asks its members to take their painful experiences and feelings and to announce them publicly, over and over again. In an ironic reversal, what once was hidden is exposed and applauded: in OA it is the most extreme stories of hitting rock bottom that receive the loudest cheers. For in OA you don't have to be young or beautiful or rich or slim or successful to have an audience and to be applauded—all you have to do is observe OA ritual.

The talent show that concluded the OA convention at the Concord Hotel provides a neat example of this principle. After staying up through a marathon weekend of group sessions, several thousand members dressed in formal evening gowns and, fortified with cans of Tab, crowded into the hotel's large theater, which only the week before had featured Shirley MacLaine. But now, any OA member who had signed up to perform became a star.

There were no auditions and no selections. Indeed, what was most impressive about the show was that the performances were so unrehearsed and unpolished. One after another, women with unremarkable voices got up in front of thousands to sing original lyrics of hope and recovery to the tunes of "Climb Every Mountain" and "Born Free." One after another tried to stir the audience into exultation at the ability of the human spirit to transcend troubles and pain, and to rejoice that the seemingly impossible could be accomplished.

One of the most moving performances was given by a woman who came on stage dressed in a tuxedo. Seating herself on a stool, she began by telling jokes. But soon her jokes dissolved into hysterical tears as she talked about her deceased father and his fruit store. For the rest of the time allotted to her act she cried and talked about how she used to help her father in the fruit store, how much she loved and missed him, and how she wished he could see her now.

This performance, like all the others, drew emotional applause from the audience of thousands. For what was being applauded was not any talent but rather the fact that in OA even such a person as this could get up on stage and be listened to. What was applauded was that everyone, no matter what the quality of her performance by conventional standards, could have her moment of attention, respect, and even glory.

3

Summer Diet Camp: A Brief Transformation

Girl Camper: Adele, is toothpaste fattening? Because some kids are eating it.

Adele (Camp Owner and Director): Very nice. Now what does that tell you?

Second Girl Camper: (Shouts out, laughing) It tells you that we're hungry.

Adele: No, it doesn't tell me you're hungry. It tells me that you are obsessed with eating and that's all you think about.

Camp Laurel, which used to be a motel, consists of two dozen bungalows arranged in a circle around a concrete driveway. In the middle of the circle is a dirt playground with swings, seesaws, and a turning platform.

For the hundreds of fat children who have been sent here for the summer to lose weight, the camp represents many contradictory things: a prison, a refuge, a place to be transformed.

Camp Laurel is attended by children and teenagers, both male and female, from ages seven to eighteen, and by older counselors who have also come to lose weight. Although some of the children are very heavy (100 pounds or more overweight)

49

others are barely plump, and certainly not more than five or
ten pounds overweight. Most are from Jewish middle-class
families. The cost for each camper will come close to $1,800.
Throughout the summer each will be restricted to a daily diet
of under twelve hundred calories and forced to exercise as
much as possible.

We can already see among these campers the early stages
of life themes glimpsed earlier in NAAFA and Overeaters
Anonymous. It is well known that the great majority (80 to 90
percent) of fat children become fat adults. But as early as
childhood we can also see the beginnings of experiences and
world views that will probably follow the overweight person
all through life: being excluded and separated from normal
society because of their weight, believing that losing weight
will solve all their problems, and experiencing dieting as unjust
punishment imposed from the outside.

"Girls Bunks one through four, and Boys three through
nine, get to the dining hall, *now!* Judy Cohen come to the
office for a phone call. David Goodman report to your bunk."

It is noontime, and the camp owner's voice booms over the
loudspeaker, reaching every corner of the grounds. The voice
comes often. There is rarely more than five minutes of respite
from the loudspeaker.

The announcement that it is time to eat is hardly necessary,
for as usual, lunch has been eagerly anticipated all morning,
and speculations about what will be served have dominated
talk around the camp for the past two hours. But as the children
file through the food line, collect their portions, and take places
with their bunk-mates at the long tables and benches, their
fantasies dissolve before the paltry meal. Lunch today is a slice
of bologna and a slice of American cheese on a single thin
piece of white bread, a small portion of canned mandarin or-
anges, washed of their syrup, and served in a little accordion
paper cup (the size used at lunch counters to serve mayonnaise),
four ounces of reconstituted instant nonfat milk mixed with
artificial sweetener, and a small serving of iceberg lettuce
topped with a ring of green pepper. The meal is served on
paper plates and eaten with plastic utensils.

While they silently eat, more information comes over the
loudspeaker, and one girl is sent out of the dining hall for
talking to her neighbor before the announcements are completed. Although they have been instructed to eat slowly, lunch

is finished in ten minutes and soon the campers congregate in small groups in the playground outside. Reminiscing about the foods they used to eat, their faces and voices becoming animated once again.

"My mother makes them with *both* chocolate chips and butterscotch bits," boasts one camper. "Does your mother make them with nuts?" counters another. Across the playground a camper recalls the "s'mores" they used to serve at the camp she went to the previous summer and still another proudly announces that the very block she lives on in Manhattan's Upper West Side has a Baskin-Robbins ice cream parlor and both a Barton's and Barricini's candy store.

What makes diet camp seem so much like prison is that by being sent there, the child is implicitly told that he or she is not fit to be with normal children. And although some eventually come to believe (or partly believe) that they are being sent for their own good, few are happy about it at first. Not only does the experience segregate fat children from the world of normals, but it also takes a happy time—summer—and turns it into a season of deprivation and labor. It denies these children what they most enjoy doing—eating—and substitutes what they hate most: strenuous exercise. Several campers lie to their winter friends about where they are going for the summer, because they are ashamed and feel that being sent to a special camp will further mark them as fat and different in the eyes of their peers.

Some of the younger children are first-timers to the camp and are especially upset at the news of being sent there. Several are hardly overweight but have parents who are fat and want to make sure their children won't be. Indeed, one slightly overweight ten-year-old recalls that her mother forced her to come. The girl had no part in the decision, even though when the camp brochures arrived in the mail, she ripped them up and ran to her room, threatening to leave home.

Not only do the children feel constantly starved for food (and indeed, one might well ask whether young children should be on such a restricted diet) but to some extent they also regard the staff as jailers. The presumption is made by the staff that without constant surveillance many of the children will be importing forbidden food into the camp, cheating on their diets, and avoiding exercise. The enforcement of diets and exercise is both a cause and outcome of the children's noncompliance.

Feeling pushed around, the children do rebel wherever they can. Complaining of how the camp is "killing them," many approach exercises and sports that children usually enjoy with a lethargy and disdain that is remarkable. And excuses for sitting out activities are made so frequently that the counselors quite rightly argue, "Girls, you can't be having your period for a month at a time." The counselors also calculate that if all the complained-of ailments were legitimate, roughly a quarter of the camp children might be considered badly injured at any given time. This is difficult to believe, considering the care with which the children move themselves.

But most rebellious of all are the food smugglers. Dreaming up ways to cheat on the diet is a continuous project among campers, pursued with far more interest and enthusiasm than the exercises. The camp has a fairly tight food control system. For example, all packages arriving in the mail must be opened in a counselor's presence, and even money is forbidden to campers since it might be used to commission the purchase of candy when someone gets permission to go into town. The camp expects this mutiny from the diet. The older children know that all campers are sent to the movies the afternoons after parents' visiting days so their bunks and mattresses can be thoroughly searched by counselors for hidden food.

Finally, many campers are cynical about whose interests are served by camp policies. While they do not believe that they are really the victims of staff cruelty (most of the campers think the counselors, being fat themselves, are sympathetic) they do suspect that the profit motive rather than concern for their welfare is behind most of the policies. For example, when some campers petitioned for a higher ration of protein in their diet they were skeptical of the camp owner's explanations: that she served such foods as cereal for breakfast because the children would always be exposed to foods like these, and needed to learn how to eat them in modified portions.

The children's skepticism is logical. Many have attended the camp during previous summers and always regained the lost weight by New Year's. And many admit that even though they want to lose weight, if left free of external control, they would be eating fattening foods.

What ultimately undermines their faith in the camp and makes it seem even more like a prison is the hypocrisy of the staff. The counselors are supposed to be role models for the campers in diet and exercise, but they frequently show the smallest weight losses. It is obvious why: they are allowed into town so they have more opportunities to cheat. Despite their presumed greater maturity the counselors illustrate the principle that once external control is removed, many will abandon the diet.

Furthermore, the camp owner herself is overweight, and though her lectures are wise and she is the object of some affection from the campers, she, too, is considered a hypocrite. Because she allowed some of the "homesick" campers to come to her house (on the camp grounds) and do chores like make her bed, they have had opportunities to observe her own eating habits. Word got around and now campers complain that "Adele doesn't practice what she preaches. She eats half a cherry pie and washes it down with nonfat milk." Other children gossip about how she has not one, but *two* refrigerators in her kitchen and how one is always filled with ice cream and cake.

If the children are cynical about the ultimate benefits of the diet camp, so are the staff and management. Asked whether the camp could be the subject of a story in the media, the top administrators considered among themselves whether they had anything to lose by this kind of coverage. One administrator speculated, "Well, they could say that 95 percent of diets fail and people gain the weight back, but even if they do say it, that can't hurt us. All the parents who send their children here think their kids will be one of the 5 percent."

One of the most significant dangers of sending children to a diet camp is that they learn to associate dieting with punishment or at least arbitrary external rule rather than as something voluntarily pursued as a way of being good to themselves. The source of control for what can or can't be eaten rests outside the child, and the child's sense of control can then come only from cheating or resisting. Thus begins a long career of associating dieting with oppressive restrictions imposed from the outside and to be resisted or abandoned. Thus the camp may be experienced as a prison in a fundamental way; put someone in prison and all they will think about is how to get out. Put people on a diet with external monitors and enforcement and all they will think about is how to cheat. What campers may be learning, like first-time offenders in jail, may be why they should resent the authorities and how to circumvent them rather than why and how they should "rehabilitate" themselves.

Of course, the children at Camp Laurel complain in the same ways that children always complain about camp: that the management is repressive, that there aren't enough good activities, that the food is terrible. Slender children at regular camps, too, often feel that camp is like a prison and fight with the staff about unfair rules. The difference between Camp Laurel and the others is that for the fat children struggles with authority are centered around food and dieting, just as fat adults often focus exclusively on weight as the cause of their troubles.

It would be very mistaken, however, to think that Camp Laurel represents merely a prison for its residents. It is also a refuge from a hostile world. Although children new to the camp may at first resent being sent, many come to like it. Some of the older children even come of their own choice. For them, Camp Laurel is a last resort, all other diets having failed. Some already feel excluded from the world of normal teenagers, so the camp represents a friendly, comfortable home rather than bitter exile.

Having acknowledged that they are indeed fat, many children find pleasure in being with others of their own kind. It is often said at Camp Laurel that the kids there are "nicer" than children at regular camps. Indeed, given the teasing and exclusion these children would probably experience among slim children, this is probably true. Many children also remark that only among other fat children could they feel comfortable enough to wear bathing suits, shorts, and halters and participate in sports and physical activities.

Many are relieved to learn that others use the very same lies and deceits they have used to obtain and eat forbidden foods. Others are comforted in discovering that others have suffered through the same fights with parents and humiliations in gym class or embarrassment from being unable to keep up with other children in physical activities. In the special world of the camp, their sensitivity about weight is even reduced enough for some to willingly adapt to fat-associated nicknames such as Blimp or Stubby—names they would never tolerate in the outside world.

Learning to be comfortable around other fat children is just one of the many identity experiences children have at camp. In some ways, being with other fat children minimizes the salience of their weight for their social identities. Since all the children are fat, they can see and relate to each other and themselves in terms of other characteristics. But in other ways being segregated from the normal world also underscores and enlarges the importance of their weight. In an ironic way the camp actually schools them in the ways of surviving as a fat person in a hostile, unsympathetic world and, indeed, teaches them to view the world from the perspective of a member of an oppressed minority group. Whether the camp is considered a refuge or a prison, one thing is certain: the outside world is a place to be dealt with guardedly. A much-talked-about camp episode that occurred during the summer illustrates this point.

During an athletic meet between Camp Laurel and a neighboring (regular) boys' camp, the Laurel boys were successfully baited by their adversaries. While the counselors weren't around, the "normal" boys taunted the fat children with Oreo cookies. Dangling the cookies before them, the thinner boys teased, "Here, doggie. Have a cookie, doggie." Starved for long-missed sweets and not knowing when they would have such an opportunity again, the Laurel boys gratefully grabbed the cookies and ate them.

In a camp meeting that followed this event, the camp owner lectured about the disgrace the campers had brought on themselves by eating the cookies. This was placed in the context of reminding the children that they must always remember their disadvantaged position in the world:

Adele: They weren't being friendly when they offered you cookies. They don't look at you the way we see ourselves. Thin people look at us differently. They don't understand us. When they offered you food it was like offering food to the animals at the zoo. They are offering you food as a big joke and they are laughing *at* you, not with you.

Despite the lethargy and occasional cheating, and the doubtfulness of the camp's program as a long-term solution, most of the children do lose a substantial amount of weight (over 20 pounds) during the summer. For the smaller ones, this amount of weight loss can transform a fat child into a slim one. Moreover, since the children are separated from their families and friends all summer, the change in appearance takes on the dramatic character of a life transformation.

If food is one of the main topics of conversation among campers, losing weight is the other. Over the weeks as they lose weight they constantly ask one another, "If you saw me on the street and you didn't know me, would you think I was fat?" Undaunted by their previous experiences of gaining back lost weight, they frequently vow that this will be their last year at the camp and that they are confident of the future: "When I lose weight, I'll be *perfect*." Their exhilaration goes beyond the certainty that they will be slim, for after all, they have been raised to believe that their weight is the cause of all their unhappiness. All kinds of major benefits are expected to follow: "When I lose weight, I'll do better in school and I'll be more extroverted." Faith in the millennium even carries them through trying experiences. Said one camper, "When the kids from the other camp tease me and call me a fat pig I say, 'I may be fat, but I'm doing something about it. You're stupid; what can you do about that?' If you're ugly or stupid, you're stuck with it, but fat you can always lose."

"Half of you is missing when you go home," one camper explains. It is an interesting way to describe the transformation, for it suggests the feeling that part of their identities will be left behind with the weight that is shed. When one considers what it must feel like to come from a family where slimness is associated with upward social mobility and fatness with one's ethnic origins (as it is among many Jewish and Italian Americans), this statement has special poignancy.

The contradictory meanings and nature of the camp are nowhere better expressed than in the weekly nutrition classes held for each division. It is the time, once a week, when the campers are weighed and thus rewarded for their week's labors.

The owner of the camp starts each class by reading the "ideal" weights for every height represented in the group, and the children listen, transfixed, asking her to repeat the weights over and over again. A few argue with the "ideal" and point out that individual build should be taken into account, and to this point Adele always agrees. One boy can be heard complaining, "According to that chart I should lose 15 more pounds. If I lost another 15 pounds I'd be *dead*."

One nutrition class for the twelve-year-old girls got under way when Adele invited them to raise problems or questions:

Adele: While we're waiting for the counselors to set up the scales, let me take some questions.

Girl: Adele, will I ever be able to eat cake?

Adele: I wouldn't say you can never eat cake, but you have to remember we're different from other people. Thin people only eat when they're hungry. Do you ever turn down food? After dinner, when you have company and you mother serves cake do you ever say no? Skinny people only eat when they're hungry.

There were no other questions, so Adele decided to grill them. "Let me ask *you* a question. Who can tell us all a good reason for losing weight? Raise your hand."

One small girl raised her hand and answered, "I don't *like* being fat." Another volunteered, "You're fat and people laugh at you." A third added, "You can't go places."

By now the scales were set up on the auditorium stage and the children lined up. One came running down the steps screaming and crying, "Five pounds—I lost five pounds." Tears of joy rolled down her face. Others repeated the gesture, hugging their friends and wildly jumping up and down. They seemed to mimic contestants on a television game show. One girl called to her friends, "I can't believe it—I'm in my *teens*" (meaning she weighed under 120). More quietly, another told a friend that she weighed under 200 pounds for the first time since she was ten years old.

But there were also disappointments. Some had lost only a pound or two in the last week, or perhaps only 10 pounds since camp had started four weeks earlier, and they complained that the small losses didn't justify the costs and sacrifice. Adele had an answer ready.

Adele: This is a small town and I hear everything that goes on. If you belch at the other end of town, I can hear it here. Of those of you who lost less than two pounds,

how many of you went horseback riding in town on
Tuesday?
[Several raise hands]

Adele: Of you girls, is there anyone who has something to
tell the group?
[Silence]

Adele: Doesn't anyone have anything they would like to
share?

Girl [*near tears*]: I cheated.

Adele: You what? Say it louder.

Girl: I cheated.

Adele: O.K. I knew this happened. [To the girl] Would you
tell me where you got the money to buy food?

Girl: I'm not telling.

Adele: You know it's against the rules for you to have
money, so I'm asking you where you got it.

Girl: I'm not saying.

Adele: You don't have to tell me any names—just tell me
whether it was a friend who gave you the money, or did
you steal the candy?

Girl: No, it was a friend.

Adele: That was no friend. A friend wouldn't give you
money to do something self-destructive. You might think
she's a friend, but she's not. Girls, you're just going to
have to ask yourselves what's more important to you—
eating or your self-respect.
[Silence, then another girl raises her hand]

2nd Girl: Adele, what's for lunch?

Adele: I'm not going to answer that question.

The conversation now turned to the controversial question of chewing gum. All the campers had been asked to turn in their gum, but a few had hoarded their supply and gotten caught when they threw the wrappers on the lawn. Because of this, Adele had prohibited gum for another few weeks:

Adele: Because of Dana, no one in camp will be getting gum. Come up here, Dana. Where did you get that gum?

Dana: Somebody gave it to me.

Adele: Who?

Dana: Somebody.

Adele: I want you to learn how to live with one another. You were told that until everyone stops chewing, no one will. Now, Dana, you are personally responsible for stopping everyone from chewing. How do you feel about it?

Dana: [Shrugs her shoulders].

Adele: You don't care.

Because parents' visiting day was coming up soon, and the campers would be going out for the day, Adele handed out copies of sample menus from restaurants in order to drill them on what they could order.

"Okay, girls. What would be better, french fried potatoes or baked potatoes?"

In chorus, they answered back, "Baked potatoes," but a few giggled, "French fries!"

"What would be better, steak or fish?"

"Fish!"

Time was running out, but Adele had a moment for one more question. A slim girl raised her hand: "Adele, if you're on maintenance, are you allowed to eat french fries?" "Girls, I've answered that question a million times. I hate to cut this

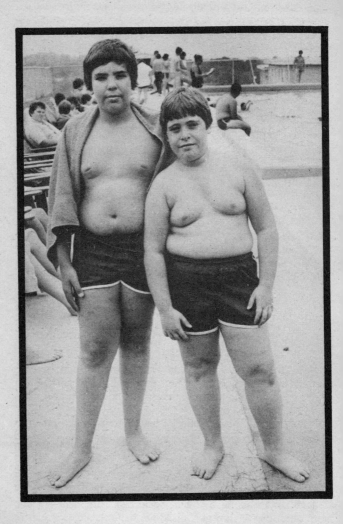

short, but the next class is waiting." As they started to file out of the room she called some final advice after them, "Girls, are you chewing your food well and eating slowly?"

Comparisons between the campers in nutrition class are inevitable. The fact that some have reached their goal and become slim and that for most this would have been impossible in one summer points out the wide range of sizes among the campers. And sadly, there are strains between the groups. For if the camp generally has the aura of a sanctuary, it is also true that some of the painful experiences the children encounter in the outside world are reproduced within the camp as well. As one of the larger fourteen-year-old girls explained, a small group of the thinnest girls in the camp formed an elite clique and made mean remarks to the fatter girls, gossiping behind their backs about what size pants the larger girls wore. According to this camper, these thin "beauties" of the camp would frequently admire themselves in the mirror while complaining, "Oh, I'm so fat," in front of the larger girls in a deliberate attempt to make them feel uncomfortable. In the view of the fatter campers, several girls of essentially normal weight had come to camp so they could feel "superior" to the others and have all the boys chasing after them.

There is some evidence to support these observations and interpretations. There are many fewer boys than girls attending Camp Laurel, and most of the boys are indeed interested in dating the slimmer girls. For example, one seventeen-year-old male counselor who was quite a bit overweight himself admitted that he preferred the thinner girls and would certainly never date a fat girl at home, because his parents had told him that he should have "the best." Fat girls, in his estimation, had no self-respect because they had to settle for what they could get. He also expressed concern about how fat girlfriends would reflect on him: "If I dated a fat girl and walked down the street, someone would say, 'Oh look at that fat couple. Aren't they cute.' But if I was with a thin girl, I wouldn't mind if someone said, 'How did that fat guy get that beautiful girl—he must be pretty good.'" Asked if he thought it was worse to be a fat woman than a fat man he replied, "A guy can be big, but a girl should be petite. Girl goes with petite like pie goes with coffee or bagels go with cream cheese."

The relationship between the slimmer and fatter girls is complicated. To the larger girls, the thin ones represent both their persecutors and also what they might become. For even though there is a division, all are on a continuum of suffering and triumph, symbolized by their ritual of trading clothes up the weight line as the campers get slimmer. As their clothes become too big, each passes the discarded items along to others who can just now fit into them. So, even if all cannot become thin over the summer, they all can experience some taste of transformation. If all do not go home transformed into "normal" children, each has had an opportunity to see herself in a different way. When their parents collect them at the end of the summer, most go home looking forward to a new life.

For many, this taste of transformation will not be enough to sustain their weight loss. Even on visiting day, it is already obvious that the transformation is only skin deep, and once free of external control they will revert to their old habits. Despite what they learned in nutrition class and even in the presence of their parents, many go on a binge, jamming so much eating into their day-long furlough that they actually make themselves sick with indigestion after weeks of dieting. And like paroled prisoners who go back to the old neighborhood, once on the loose at the end of summer many of the campers will reacquaint themselves with all their old friends: pizza, ice cream, candy, and french fries. Many will be back at Camp Laurel the next summer.

4

Set Apart:
The Fat Person
as an
Antisocial Figure

A common and important point is made by NAAFA, OA, and children's diet camps, despite their differences: the very existence of each organization is evidence of how fat persons are isolated and set apart from "normal" society. But why does this happen? What sentiments and reactions do fat people arouse in others that would make them respond so negatively? A few clues to this puzzle can be found in some stories told to me by a friend (a woman of average size) who described her reactions to some very fat women she saw in public settings.

Walking through a store, my friend Barbara recently found herself staring at the massive arms (bared by a sleeveless dress) of a woman who weighed over 300 pounds. To Barbara's eyes this flesh was so white, so spongy that she thought, "She must spend all of her time at home, growing herself like a mushroom." In this case, my friend associated the size and texture of the woman's flesh with a deep willfulness and self-absorption. She also recalled a different reaction to another fat woman.

Riding a bus that runs from San Francisco to Palo Alto, Barbara one day became both fascinated and repelled by the sight of a hugely fat passenger. Asked how old the woman was, my friend shrugged her shoulders, as if to say the woman's massive size had somehow made her age either irrelevant or indeterminable, but finally she placed the woman somewhere in her thirties. What had impressed her was the woman's dress.

She had obviously made it for herself out of a bedspread. The pattern of the material was very large, and Barbara noted with some interest that the bold pattern seemed appropriate given the size of the dress and the woman. The woman was carrying two vinyl suitcases, one in each hand (she appeared to be returning from a trip) and my friend thought the luggage looked like little wings on a giant beetle.

The woman manuevered herself and the suitcases with obvious difficulty. Rather than move very far into the bus she sat in a front seat reserved for the elderly and the physically handicapped. Both Barbara and the fat passenger rode to the same suburban station, where each placed a telephone call for someone to pick them up. Barbara, still curious about the fat woman, was surprised that she dialed a number from memory, as if to a husband or another very close, for she had imagined during the bus ride that this woman must lead an isolated life.

Barbara at first had felt great pity for how hard the woman's life must have been. Thinking about what it must be like to have to make one's own dresses out of bedspreads, or to have such trouble moving about and carrying packages, my friend imagined that being fat must have cost this woman tremendous effort and energy. But her pity had soon turned into anger at what she believed the woman was doing to herself by being so fat. She wanted to shake the woman, to tell her to pull herself together.

Other of my friends have admitted a similar anger at fat people because they take up more than a fair share of space. In their eyes, fat people seem to aggressively intrude themselves beyond proper boundaries. This reaction corresponds with criticisms appearing with increasing frequency in newspapers that fat people use up too many resources. Claims are made by Blue Cross and government officials that obese people drive up the cost of health care and nutritionists admonish that fat people eat enough excess food to fuel several American cities. Another friend recalled that when she was recently at the airport she saw a man who must have weighed 400 pounds. He was chain-smoking and sweating profusely. My friend thought, "This man is killing himself, and we're all going to pay for it."

Such depth of feeling is puzzling. It is somewhat understandable that fat people might be resented for driving up health costs (although the costs due to obesity are miniscule compared, say, with the costs of cancer caused by environmental and occupational hazards or the enormous profits of the health industry). But the health-cost argument is a paltry explanation for the sentiments aroused. A person with heart disease who smokes or works too hard may be criticized by friends for his habits, but he does not inspire the horror, loathing, speculation, repugnance, and avoidance that very fat people do.

Perhaps mere visibility plays a part. Some would argue that smoking doesn't make a person physically unattractive, but fat does. Even so, there is more to the process of perceiving fat people as characters who are disturbingly unresponsive to social control.

Being slim is highly valued in our society. A fat person violates that value and therefore offends society's expectations. This is especially true for women, whose worth and achievement are judged largely on the basis of how they look. And when expectations are violated, explanations and interpretations inevitably follow. Because of these further interpretations, the fat person's differentness comes to be perceived as more than physical.

Responses vary according to the perspective of the viewer. People who used to be fat or fear gaining weight often confess to a sense of horror when they see an obese person. The dreaded "lack of self-control" lurks perhaps in themselves. Those who were never fat and can't imagine becoming so often project onto fat people a willful laziness and self-indulgence. How could a person "let herself go" like that? But in both cases the interpretation that the fat person is uncontrolled (whether from weakness or defiance) lurks behind the reactions of loathing and horror.

Furthermore, by its very nature deviance has a tendency to become generalized: once a person is perceived as deviant at all, nothing about her is trusted or taken for granted, and the trait that distinguishes her seems to color her entire being in the eyes of others. As the stories of fat people vividly demonstrate, being overweight and the interpretations made of it wind up affecting all of a person's life, pushing the fat person into a special, marginal relationship to the world. Frequently she is clearly excluded, but even when included with others there is always tension, qualification, uncertainty, self-consciousness, and uneasiness between herself and "normals." Are others thinking about her weight? Indeed, she wonders, too,

how far she can go in claiming the rights and privileges of
"normal" human beings, and where she must not presume to
cross the line.

Our earliest experience of social conventions and control
is in the family. For many fat people, the family was the first
social setting where their weight defined them as deviant, ab-
normal, and problematic. Fat children often struggle with their
parents over food and eating. Conflict over eating habits is of
course common among all American parents and children, but
in the case of fat children the arguments take on added significance and eating becomes closely associated with autonomy, control, and love. Shirley Kaufman, a forty-seven-year-
old clinical psychologist, tells her story this way:

> My father died when I was five, and my mother never
> remarried. She worked in a factory, and we were fairly
> poor...
>
> My main act of rebellion was my refusal to eat, and
> we struggled until I was seven or eight about it. She [my
> mother] would force-feed me, and I would vomit...
>
> For a Jewish mother, refusing to eat and vomiting the
> food was the way to get to her—it really bothered her.
> She would always threaten to send us to an orphanage—
> or tell us she would die and we would have to go to an
> orphanage.
>
> The big treat in our house was certain kinds of cake.
> We got desserts on weekends largely because she loved
> them—Charlotte Russes and something called Mucatars—
> cakes with whipped cream.
>
> I didn't particularly like whipped cream. I always
> loved chocolate, and she never got us that (since she
> didn't like it), so I would steal it. By the time I was
> twelve I was concerned about my weight. Between the
> ages of twelve and fifteen I'd be careful and fast all day
> Saturday until the late afternoon and then I would go to
> the candy store and have a chocolate sundae *without*
> whipped cream. My mother would be furious that I
> wouldn't eat her food all day.

This woman (like several others I interviewed) has throughout her life used food and weight to assert and feel control in

her relationships and her place in the world. And when these assertions run against the wishes of parents or husband, eating and weight become associated with a refusal to bow to social control. Joan Bauer, a thirty-six-year-old physics professor, has lately realized that her mother used food and feeding to coerce her children and her family, though it had appeared on the surface that her father was the dominant parent:

Once I was fat my mother's efforts to help me became sources of great pain for me because there were constant struggles about my being "good," which took all my energy, and then I would collapse from not being able to tolerate being good anymore, and then I would sneak and there would be confrontations.

My mother is very controlling about food generally and . . . she doesn't like people trespassing on her turf with regard to food. She runs a tight kitchen and also has tight standards about food value. I watch her with my children and I get an instant replay of my childhood. The "don't eat cookies before dinner" thing which every parent struggles with gets elevated into a really big deal, and I feel like saying to her, "Mother—all right, so let him have a cookie. It's not worth this kind of rigidity. I don't want to listen to him cry for twenty minutes—so what if he doesn't eat so much dinner?"

I watch the rigidity with which she prevents my kids from eating—partly because she wants her meal appreciated, partly because she wants to be in control of the stuff that's in her domain, partly because she has legitimate concerns about nutrition, and partly because food is one of the places where she expresses her very great needs to control the world around her.

For me fatness is the only area in my life where I've allowed myself to relinquish control, to be irrational and crazy, counterproductive, be rebellious against my family. This is the one place I let myself act like an ass. I never do in intellect, social life, parenting, financial management. You name it—I'm good at it. I'm responsible and dependable, damn it. With food I am an idiot. The *blob* of uncontrolled craziness. And it's clear to me that when I was trying to fast I worked at being irrational and foolish and unproductive in other areas to take some of the heat off the need to be indulgent in relation to food.

A graphic description of how being fat may come to symbolize the child's rebelliousness toward her parents is found in the novel *Lady Oracle* by Margaret Atwood. The narrator and heroine of the story (now a successful writer) attempts throughout the novel to escape from her hidden past identities, including her fat childhood, which was spent at war with her mother:

> By this time I was eating steadily, doggedly, stubbornly, anything I could get. The war between myself and my mother was on in earnest; the disputed territory was my body. I didn't quite know this, though I sensed it in a hazy way; but I reacted to the diet booklets she left on my pillow, to the bribes of dresses she would give me if I would reduce to fit them . . . to her cutting remarks about my size, to her pleas about my health . . . to the specialists she sent me to and the pills they prescribed, to all of these things, with another Mars bar or a double helping of french fries. I swelled visibly, relentlessly, before her very eyes; I rose like dough, my body advanced inch by inch towards her across the dining-room table, in this at least I was undefeated. I was five feet four and still growing, and I weighed a hundred and eighty-two pounds. . . .
> I finished the slab of leftover cake and rose to my feet, my stomach bumping the table. . . . I had developed the habit of clomping silently but very visibly through rooms in which my mother was sitting; it was a sort of fashion show in reverse, it was a display, I wanted her to see and recognize what little effect her nagging and pleas were having.[1]

To parents a fat child is an embarrassment, being viewed by society as a poor reflection on the parents themselves. If obesity is an expression of something gone wrong with the child, there must be something wrong with the parents as well, and the way they treated the child. Until adolescence, children are not regarded as responsible, so fat children are pitied and their parents blamed. Many parents therefore not only fight bitterly with their overweight children about their eating habits but also (like the parents of NAAFA member Laura Campbell) let their children know that they are embarrassed and repelled by them. However much some children may experience triumph in defying their parents with eating, they are also devastated by their parents' repugnance. Knowing that even their parents are ashamed to be seen with them is an early and most powerful experience for fat people. These feelings were nicely captured on an episode of CBS TV's "Magazine Show" in an interview with the family of a fat teenage girl. The girl explained that her mother had stopped taking her places. When asked by the interviewer if she was embarrassed by her overweight daughter, the mother refused to answer the question, whereupon the father cut in: "The answer is: of course we're embarrassed. And we try to communicate in this family. I've said to her, 'We're not proud of the way you look; don't expect us to pretend we are.'"

But even sympathetic parents, sincerely proud of their child, cannot assuage the feelings of differentness and inferiority a fat child sees reflected in the eyes of peers. For a girl this problem of course grows as the child reaches puberty and adolescence and is increasingly evaluated for acceptability in mixed-sex activities. As one teenage girl observed, a complicated set of strains existed between herself and her slim friends as they let her know that they really didn't want her to come on a weekend outing:

> How would it look to go on a long weekend of orgies with me unless I were coming along as the chaperone? Their judgment of only half-telling me about the weekend was because I wasn't pretty enough to make it with the guys—who'd want to dance sexy with me? They kept saying that I might not have the right casual clothes to go, but I knew my body wouldn't pass their test. Doris said it was for my own good if I didn't go with them because people would make me feel sad by staring at me—especially my big stomach and I wasn't pregnant. It wouldn't be any fun for me to come along just to watch, they said, and I had to face it that the guys might not be turned on to me with 30 extra pounds so I would feel left out. The gang worked hard to convince me what a

miserable time I would have on the weekend, including
how embarrassed I'd feel about eating. They kept saying
that it wasn't that they didn't want me to come—they
were trying to protect me. This made me feel bad and I
realized I'd spoil their fun if I went—they didn't want to
keep seeing a fat freak around them.[2]

It is not simply the "dating" question that excludes fat children. Being victimized by other children and always the last
to be chosen for any team, they often turn to solitary activities.
They become readers. They befriend adults. Indeed, many fat
children experience a premature or precocious adulthood.
Many women who were fat as children recall that their mothers
treated them as peers or confidants rather than children. The
loss of childhood and the failure to fit in is further dramatized
by clothes—the fat child can't even fit into children's sizes and
must often wear clothes made for adults.

When the marginality of the fat child becomes even more
pronounced at puberty, as dating and male and female gender
roles become more salient, some adaptations characteristically
arise in the lives of fat girls. One is to become precociously
"sexy." Many overweight women develop secondary sexual
characteristics earlier than their friends, and look older than
their real age because of their size. This leads to older boys
or men treating them as sexual beings earlier than other girls
their age. Others befriend boys rather than girls, becoming
"one of the boys," since they are not regarded by either boys
or girls as "regular" girls. And probably the most common
adaptation of all is for the fat adolescent girl to take on the
role of the desexualized but sympathetic "listener" or chaperone
for other girls:

I had a terrific personality and my friends were nice
girls, the kind boys wanted to take out to dances and
movies, where they would be seen in public and admired.
These girls liked to walk home with me, asking my
advice and confiding in me, for two reasons: if a boy
who was not wanted approached them, there I was, a fat
duenna, the perfect excuse, it was like having your own
private tank; and if a more desirable boy turned up, how
could my friends help but look good beside me? In
addition, I was very understanding, I always knew the

right moment to say, "See you tomorrow," and vanish into the distance like a blimp in a steady wind, leaving the couple gazing at each other on the sidewalk in front of those trim Braeside houses, those clipped lawns. The girls would phone me up later, breathlessly, and say, "Guess what happened," and I would say, "Oh, what?" as though I were thrilled and delighted and could hardly wait to find out. I could be depended on not to show envy, not to flirt competitively, and not to wonder why I wasn't invited to the mixed-couples parties of these, my dearest friends. Though immersed in flesh, I was regarded as being above its desires, which of course was not true.[3]

But even when a child assumes a special role, such as confidante, and so creates a place for herself in the social world, her position is still defined by her weight. Even if not completely isolated, her participation is marginal and partial and her experience vicarious. As the confidante she knows life only from the distance of an observer. And, her marginality and separation is increased because she is always self-conscious about her weight, always wondering what others are thinking about it while not really wanting to know.

In trying to decide what they may and may not risk, many fat people experience life as double jeopardy. In every situation they must guess whether or not others view them as deviant.

If they presume that others see them as normal and act like a normal person (for example, getting up to dance at a party or eating a non-dietetic meal or acting flirtatiously) they run the risk of being called ridiculous. On the other hand, if they never take the risk of presenting themselves as normal, they relinquish any chance of ratification, of participating in the world and its pleasures.

These are hard decisions. They are never made once and for all. Each new social contact, each action committed in public, no matter how trivial or superficial, is dominated by the fat person's concerns about how she appears to others. Thus her participation in the world is often tentative and filled with fear of being discovered, labeled as the freak she fears herself to be. Here from her unpublished autobiography are the memories of Ellin, a young woman who was always 25 to 50 pounds overweight during her college years and in her twenties:

I could never really buy what I wanted in the store. I would always think the cashier would know that I was a compulsive eater, when they saw the candy, the cookies, the ice cream. I would go to different stores so that I wouldn't keep seeing the same sales people. I was always ashamed in front of the young male clerks at the delicatessen. If I went to a bakery, that was very problematic: you have to carry the box in the street. If it's just food in a brown bag, no one knows, but everyone knows what's inside the cake box. Sometimes I would tell them to put it in a bag, risking getting the eclairs crushed rather than having someone see me carry the box. Or I would take a taxi so I wouldn't have to walk in the street with the box. I would think: they know I'm not buying it for a family because I'm buying one of each kind instead of six eclairs. I would make up questions: do you think this is enough for four people, so they wouldn't think it was just for me. Sometimes I would have to start eating it in the taxi, even though I knew the taxi driver would think I was a slob. Once a taxi driver said, "Hey, isn't that fattening?" And I was horrified. But I had to eat it in the taxi because I was going to someone's house and I couldn't eat it there.

. . . I always felt, when I went into some boutique, that all the salegirls were staring at me and snickering, knowing that nothing in the store would fit me. I always had to say, "I'm just looking." I was terrified that someone would come into the dressing room. Since they knew that the clothes I took into the dressing room wouldn't fit and since I knew it, I always had to find some excuse when I came out as to why I wasn't going to buy them.

I always felt that the first thing anyone would notice is that I was fat. And not only that I was fat, but that they would know *why* I was fat. They would know I was neurotic, that I was unsatisfied, that I was a pig, that I had problems. They could tell immediately that I was out of control. I always looked around to see if there was anyone as fat as me. I always wondered when I saw a fat woman, "Do I look like *that?*"

. . . I felt clumsy and huge. I felt that I would knock

over furniture, bump into things, tip over chairs, not fit
into VWs, especially when people were trying to crowd
into the back seat. I felt like I was taking over the whole
room. I could never not be noticed.

I felt disgusting and like a slob. In the summer I felt
hot and sweaty, and I knew people saw my sweat as
evidence that I was too fat.

. . . I don't think I was ever willing to look ugly
although I thought of being fat as being ugly. People
have always said I had a beautiful face and "if you'd
only lose weight you'd be really beautiful." I never really
let myself go. I never got to 200 pounds. I always
thought about the way I dressed, I wore a lot of makeup
for a long time. I used to think I was totally crazy: here I
would go to great lengths putting on false eyelashes and
plucking my eyebrows when I weighed 165!

If the fat person is uncertain about how much she can get
away with in trying to "pass" for normal, then so are the people
around her uneasy, thinking always about her weight but feeling
guilty, defensive, or conflicted about letting her know it. In
many ways, weight becomes a taboo topic, a river that can't
be crossed between the fat person and others.

Sometimes the fat person feels an obligation to break the
ice by being the first to mention her weight. She may make
a point of saying that she is dieting, that she would like to lose
weight. These are ways of bridging the gap, of showing others
that she sees things the way they do, that she is trying to
observe the rules. Conversely, some fat people are so sensitive
and humiliated about being fat that they treat the subject of
weight as unmentionable and lose all composure when it is
brought up by someone else. If they lose weight, they are
ambivalent about having people notice, for they are both glad
of the compliments and humiliated that their former obesity
had really been silently noticed all along:

I fasted last year and went from 250 pounds to 170
during the school year. I was a little embarrassed about
it, and by and large I didn't admit to people that I was
fasting. For example, when I would go out to lunch with
people as I often did, in the early stages (I got more
public in the end when people raved about how terrific I

looked) I would lie and say, "I don't feel good, I'll just have some tea." Or I'd say "I had a late breakfast; I'm not hungry." I was uncomfortable in acknowledging that I was fat. I didn't want it to be part of the conversational domain.

Gradually I began telling more people and now most people know I fasted. When people remarked on my losing weight I felt embarrassed and intruded upon and also pleased. In fact it made me mad when in the first month no one commented when I lost 30 pounds but I told myself, well, you're so fat 30 pounds does not make much difference. (Joan Bauer)

Being fat may so dramatically dominate the image of fat women that all other "normal" or even superior traits seem to disappear from attention. Joan Bauer, the physicist quoted above, provides a good example. Because of her remarkable research she had a national reputation even as a graduate student, and was pursued by many leading universities when she was ready to take her first academic job. She wound up taking a tenured, senior position (practically unheard of for a new Ph.D.) in the department where she had been a student. During her last year of graduate study she was pregnant and gave birth to her second child. It had been an upsetting pregnancy, filled with apprehension that her obesity (she was five feet ten and weighed 250 pounds at full term) would endanger her own life or the baby's. Her doctors had given her a hard time about her weight and, already feeling sensitive about her size, she had feared that being pregnant would surely make her look ridiculous. During that year she attended a party:

I went to a physics department party that was part of my interview for my job, so the party was in my honor, but a very humiliating thing happened. This was in early March and I had had the baby three months before, during Christmas of that school year. At the party two different faculty members asked me when the baby was due. One of the things that had happened during this last weight gain was that I developed this terrific pouch on my stomach and it had overlapping, hanging fat—so I know I looked pregnant. But I was mortified. How do you answer the question, when is the baby due, when you've already had it? They didn't know me really well—only that I was the one who was so smart that was pregnant. Of course, they were embarrassed when I said I had already had the baby. They just said "I'm sorry" and then people tried to make other conversation.

A friend of mine and her husband were with me at this party and on the way home I said how mortified I had felt about this exchange and my friend said "Yes, yes I know," and her husband said, "Well, Joan, how can you expect anybody to think anything else when you have this awful cancerous-looking growth on the front of you?" My friend was furious with her husband and I've never forgiven him. He's a therapist. She later told me she yelled at him and he said that the only way to deal with something I'm so tense about is to bombard me and make it so ridiculous I have to laugh. All right, he had too much to drink and he's the caustic type, but it was a terrible thing to say.

Inexperienced and unpracticed in the social graces, a fat person is often unsure of how to interpret other people's gestures and words. While most people have a clearer self-image and pretty well know what to make of other people's behavior, the fat person is too self-conscious and too marginal to count on the accuracy of her interpretations. She reasonably comes to doubt her judgments about social situations. Joan Bauer describes how during a period of separation from her husband she was unsuccessful in meeting other men:

It was very painful for me because even where I thought there were sexual signals it always turned out that I had been wrong. When I would make a move, the man would always wind up saying overtly or covertly "You must be crazy, I don't feel that way about you." I always ended up just feeling humiliated, foolish, wondering how I could be so stupid as to think the man was attracted to me.

. . . I think my weight hasn't had much impact on my relations with colleagues because most of the people around here are pretty asexual themselves. No sexuality is projected among the male faculty here. In one sense it makes it comfortable but it's a domain of life I miss and

it pushes me further into neck-up living. But maybe the
world looks asexual to me because I'm asexual and
maybe there's flirtation and sexuality going on but people
don't relate to me that way. I do know of various
seductions of students by faculty so I put myself down
and say it's not true there's no sexuality here. It's just
that the men don't relate to me that way.

Because of all the exclusion and the tension of social life,
the fat individual often finds it easier to give up, to abandon
a world that doesn't want her anyway. She retreats instead to
the pleasures of eating in solitude. But being frozen out of the
"normal" world and labeled as deviant, everything in her pri-
vatized life takes on an illicit or furtive quality. As several
women explained, because it is pursued in secret, eating often
feels to them either like calculated, premeditated stealing, or
like engaging in a shameful perversion. And indeed, one of
the stereotypes of fat people is that they surreptitiously and
perversely substitute eating for normal human contact and even
sexuality:

Judith R.: When I would come home from parties, never
having met a man because of my weight, I would head
straight for the refrigerator to console myself for my
loneliness.

Joan Bauer: I'll do things like stay up later than anyone else
in the house so I can eat after they go to bed, even
though I know I'm not particularly hungry.

Claire Stewart: I used to buy candy bars at work and eat
them in the bathroom.

Ellin: I was forced to sneak, starting from my public image
at home of being on a diet. My stepsister, who was about
three years older than me, was incredibly thin. She was
always on a diet. So there she was eating cottage cheese,
and I couldn't eat in front of that. But later I still had the
fear of eating in public. This meant I spent a lot of time
in the house alone, and the more alone I felt the more I
ate. I was ashamed to order what I wanted in restaurants,
thinking that any public would always be staring at me.

In New York I would go out at night to delicatessens. There were about five or six near where I lived, and usually I would stop at all of them, buying something different so it wouldn't look so bad. I would usually try to buy something normal, like bananas or chicken along with the cake, the ice cream, the cookies and the candies so I wouldn't appear a total freak. I was always scared I would get mugged or raped on my way from the delicatessen, so there was that terror in addition to the terror of having to buy the food in front of all these people. I will never forget the all-night delicatessen in Sheridan Square in Greenwich Village. It was always filled with the most grotesque assortment of people you only find up at 3 A.M. in New York, and I always knew they were smirking at me as I loaded up my little cart. I used to hear them saying things about me, and I would be shaking all over as I got to the cashier, always wishing they would ring it up and get it into the bag faster.

Days when I would emerge from my apartment after eating or have to go see someone after a binge I always felt very drained and messy. It was hard to talk or be with people, thinking they must know what I had been doing. In the back of my mind I would be waiting to leave so I could get back to food. There are times I probably was never really with the people I was spending time with, because I couldn't wait to leave to get back to eating.

We started by looking at the feelings and associations that are aroused in thin people by the sight of a very fat person, and we have come full circle to the fat person's response to the world. If the society has a horror of fat people and sees them as basically antisocial characters who are greedy, secretive, isolated, or self-absorbed, and if fat people are excluded as early as childhood from the ranks of normal society, so does the fat person naturally come to feel more comfortable being alone, set apart from others, privately gratifying herself by eating. If the world treats the fat person with hostility, so does she come to feel embattled with her environment. A correspondence is constructed between the image and the reality.

5

Personal or Political: Explaining the Problems of Fat People

The philosophy of Overeaters Anonymous exemplifies a growing tendency to view obesity as a sign of emotional disturbance in the individual. In our psychologically oriented society it is increasingly assumed (especially about women) that we get fat because emotional disturbances drive us to eat compulsively. Frequently, the compulsion to overeat is suspected of being a substitute gratification for blocked, conflict-ridden, or unfulfilled desires (for sex or love, for example). Even where psychological explanations of obesity are not so fully articulated, they often color the images and assumptions that our society makes of fat people. And even where emotional causes are not assumed (for examaple, in the currently fashionable treatment mode of behavior modification, where obesity is viewed simply as the outcome of poor eating habits) it is still thought that the fat person's suffering and problems are individually based and self-produced. The solution lies in becoming slim. National diet organizations like Weight Watchers and Take Off Pounds Sensibly (TOPS) share not only the assumption that slenderizing is the answer, but also devote much group discussion time to the unconscious psychological problems that drive members to overeat.

This suspicion of underlying personal problems is not entirely unwarranted. Indeed, it is difficult to listen to overweight people without concluding that obesity, especially in an extreme form, is indeed often a symptom of unconscious conflicts or disturbances. Fat people themselves frequently have a psychological interpretation of their weight problems. Even if they don't go as far as Overeaters Anonymous in looking within for the source of their unhappiness, most feel there is something wrong with being overweight and believe their fatness to be consistent with other emotional problems they recognize. But no matter what the actual cause of obesity in any individual case, it would be difficult to be fat in our society without blaming and hating oneself, and without feeling it is a sign of something wrong. Why?

One of the appeals of Overeaters Anonymous and other diet organizations (including Weight Watchers and TOPS) is that they hold out the hope that a person can independently shape and create her own life. Most of us would like to believe that adherence to a certain program (such as a diet or a set of guiding life principles) will ease our troubles. Never mind that OA members are plagued by financial stress, illness, unemployment, divorce, and children who are drug addicts: they come to believe that they alone are responsible for the largest share of their own suffering and that they alone can achieve a solution.

This response is not without some merit. Self-improvement programs sometimes do help fulfill their potential. And if we cannot control the larger external forces that constrain and make us unhappy, we need not abandon efforts at eliminating self-induced problems. Still, it is deeply erroneous and dangerous for people to believe that all of the causes and solutions for their troubles are personal. This "illness" approach leads us inevitably to seek an individual cure. We seek in vain.

Because of the dismal failure rates of diets obesity has lately come to be viewed by the medical profession as an "incurable illness." Thus conceived (whether because of psychological or physiological disturbance) obesity, like alcoholism, takes on the character of being beyond the simple volition of the individual. Viewed in this way, obesity also becomes not quite a deliberately chosen condition, and therefore some of the guilt is removed from the individual. But viewing obesity as an illness still locates the cause of the problem and the solution for it within the individual. And ultimately, the view that fat people are sick or have real physical predispositions for their condition doesn't exempt them from contempt and blame, even within the health-care community itself.

Indeed, the health industry has recently depicted obesity as the prime symbol of our faulty "lifestyles." For example, Blue Cross recently ran advertisements in newspapers and magazines, and catchy spots on the radio, pointing the finger at overweight Americans for the high cost of health care. One full-page advertisement included an arresting sketch of an overweight man: his shirt buttons were straining, his abdomen hung sloppily over his belt. Underneath the drawing a large caption commented: "One of the reasons for the high cost of health care." Underneath the caption were graphs depicting the rise in the costs of coronary care units, implying that obesity was causing more heart attacks and therefore responsible for the rise in health costs. There was considerable distortion in this representation. There is no evidence that obesity is a major cause of heart attacks. And furthermore, the increase in coronary care unit costs is due less to a higher incidence of heart attacks (which have actually decreased in recent years), than to the proliferation of high-technology medical equipment and the profit-making activities of our health industries. The Blue Cross advertisement in question exemplifies how fat people are blamed for problems and expenses created by the structure of our medical care system and its profit orientation. Blame for the failure of the health system is shifted to individuals who are actually more its victims than its perpetrators.

This tendency is compounded by the fact that in America obesity is correlated with poverty: it is many times more prevalent among the poor than the rich and is associated with downward mobility.[1] As a "lifestyle" problem it is easy to see why obesity is a product of poverty: inexpensive convenience foods are the most fattening, and we have to be relatively wealthy to eat a high-protein diet or have the time and resources to cook healthy low-calorie meals. Access to pleasant physical exercise and athletic activities is increasingly expensive. As Overeaters Anonymous illustrates, eating is often used to dull the pain and soothe the frustrations of difficult life circumstances. While financially poor overweight people might logically be seen as the victims of social conditions that make a healthy lifestyle improbable, instead they are blamed for driving up the cost of health care and using up too many resources. It is a case of blaming the victim.

It is precisely in the area of "lifestyle" illnesses (alcoholism, drug addiction, and now "food abuse") that traditional American medicine has been least successful. These illnesses are often caused by chronic stressful life conditions and therefore don't lend themselves well to treatment by the high-technology, high-profit, acute-intervention medical care preferred by physicians and the health industries. Since they are unresponsive and unattractive to medical practice, these "lifestyle" illnesses and their treatment have largely been left to nonmedical self-help organizations, which have consequently received uncharacteristic endorsement by the medical profession.

Although obesity is viewed as an illness, most medical insurance excludes treatment for obesity unless diabetes or hypertension are involved. Thus fat patients are unattractive to physicians, except those who specialize in weight reduction and have worked out a mode of "treatment" (usually a weekly allotment of questionable drugs) that allows them to see patients in large enough volume to compensate for the relatively small fee that can be collected for each visit. It is a treatment mode well designed for the constraints of a noninsured condition.

Clearly, in its extreme form, obesity is deleterious to health. But for most people (especially women) it is concern about physical appearance, and not health, that motivates dieting. Yet few diets achieve long-term weight loss. Only about 10 percent of the patients in supervised weight-reduction programs maintain their original losses for as long as one year; after two years the percentage drops to 6 percent, then lower.[2] And there is little health benefit in the activities of most dieters who repeatedly lose and regain weight, a stress on the body that is itself probably more unhealthy than staying overweight. Furthermore, if one considers the methods that many people use to lose weight (taking amphetamines, fasting), it becomes clear that the health motive is obviously not uppermost in the minds of dieters.

These destructive methods, moreover, are often used by women who are either not overweight at all, or only slightly so, and who certainly are not fat enough to be jeopardizing their health (most studies suggest a person needs to be 20 percent over the "ideal" for their weight to have demonstrable effects on their health). And several experts have noted that while obesity is *correlated* with hypertension, and therefore indirectly with coronary disease, there is little evidence that obesity *causes* hypertension and heart disease.[3] The important point is that our common attitudes and practices with regard to obesity cannot be reasonably explained on the basis of medical considerations.

There is another explanation—one that NAAFA has repeatedly pointed out: fat people meet with subtle and flagrant discrimination in all areas of life. And discrimination against fat people most dramatically affects groups already disadvantaged: women and the poor. One well-known study[4] of college admission rates indicated that overweight girls have only one-third the chance of being admitted to prestigious colleges as slim girls with otherwise identical records. (Teenage boys are not nearly so severely penalized for being overweight—an indication of how women are punished more than men for being overweight.)

In pointing to such examples of discrimination, NAAFA calls attention to social and political factors rather than to individual self-destructiveness as responsible for the suffering experienced by fat people. When NAAFA members talk about "coming out of the closet" in the organization and becoming comfortable about acknowledging that they are fat and discussing it, they are comparing themselves to members of other oppressed groups. Like black and gay people in earlier liberation movements, NAAFA has adopted political terminology and slogans that proclaim its members' differences from others in a neutral or positive way and in a manner that disputes the majority's view of normalcy. NAAFA uses the word *fat* rather than *obese* or *overweight* just as blacks rejected the word *Negro* and *gay* was substituted for *homosexual*. In all these cases, the motive was to discard a label that had been applied by the oppressive majority and to use instead a name originating from the minority group itself.

Nor is NAAFA alone. Recent lawsuits have begun to question the legality of weight criteria for employment or membership. These suits revolve around the civil rights and health status of fat people. It is possible that recent federal legislation requiring employment of the physically handicapped in order to qualify for federal funding (Rehabilitation Act of 1973) may have relevance for charges of discrimination by fat people. There is still debate about whether fat people are protected by this legislation. Most employers justify firing or failing to hire a fat person with the argument that he or she is physically unable to do the work of a thin person. Most employers also take the position that although they are not physically fit for the job, fat people are not truly "handicapped" because their problem is voluntary. It is around these contentions that future debates about discrimination will revolve.

As we have seen, being fat is not a "voluntary" condition to the extent that most people think. The medical profession now views obesity as relatively "incurable." There is also increasing evidence that some people have body types that are constitutionally more efficient at storing fat than others. These people gain weight eating the same diet and engaging in the same physical activities that would cause others to lose weight.[5] So far the argument that obesity is an involuntary condition has not been used a great deal in discrimination suits, because few fat people want to define themselves as physically handicapped and are therefore unlikely to seek protection under the Federal Rehabilitation Act. More often, the argument for equal employment opportunity has rested on the claim that fat people are just as competent in work as thinner people.

One administrator in charge of enforcing federal fair-employment practices and affirmative action admitted that most employers can circumvent these legal requirements. Few admit that they refuse jobs because of weight—even though this obviously happens routinely. Most overweight people, in his experience, do not even challenge weight standards and simply don't apply to be a receptionist or a worker where "front-desk appearance" is one of the criteria.

But even this administrator (who seemed genuinely sympathetic) told a revealing anecdote. He reported with amusement an incident involving a "big black woman" who filed a complaint with his office. She felt she had been rejected as a file clerk because she was black. When he called the employer to investigate the complaint he learned that the employer had brought her back to the filing area and "she got stuck between the cabinets, trapping the employer in there. She became hysterical and started screaming."

Despite ridiculing the client in this story, the administrator explained that his commission generally took the view that obesity could be considered a physical handicap and therefore come under protective legislation. In order to decide whether obesity was a physical handicap in individual cases he would ask a doctor to state whether a person might safely lose a certain amount of weight in a time period satisfactory to an employer, or if the weight problem was immutable, permanent.

More recent charges of discrimination in weight requirements have been coupled with claims of sex discrimination. One stewardess sued her former employer, Continental Airlines, for firing her because she exceeded the weight limit.[6] Initially, a judgment was found in her favor, holding that the weight standards were unconstitutional sex discrimination. This was argued, presumably, because male flight attendants were not subject to the same sanctions. A federal judge ruled subsequently, however, that federal sex discrimination laws do not forbid employers to set appearance standards. Airlines could therefore legally suspend or fire fat stewardesses as long as they treat overweight male flight attendants similarly.

Despite this ruling, the case raises fundamental questions about the legal aspects of weight requirements. It is obvious that since women are evaluated more than men on the basis of physical appearance, so do they encounter greater employment discrimination if they are fat. This point is critical because it raises the possibility for another important source for politicizing attitudes about weight, namely the women's liberation movement. Because of its size and power, the women's movement could potentially bring a political analysis of weight problems to the widest possible audience in the United States. Even more than NAAFA or the litigation about discrimination, the women's movement is in an excellent position to encourage people to examine how women and men are deeply injured and oppressed by the feelings and attitudes we have about getting or being overweight. But interestingly, the women's movement has been remarkably silent on the issue of weight, even though it has denounced the oppressiveness of other kinds of beauty standards. Indeed, it is puzzling that the pressure to be stylishly thin and the toll this takes on women has received practically no attention, save from a small number of radical feminists and lesbians who consider the issue as derivative of the more general social, political, and psychological subordination of women.

Like NAAFA, these radical feminists address the social isolation and psychological oppression of fat women, yet unlike NAAFA (which asks only that fat people be allowed to participate fully in society as it currently exists), the feminists argue that "fat oppression" is part of the larger problem of sexism in our society. Such an argument appeared in a lesbian newsletter article entitled "Looksism as Social Control":

Looksism encompasses sexism, ageism, racism and other forms of discrimination that nullify peoples' consciousness. We are in the era of packaging. The aesthetics of human beauty are the aesthetics of packaging, when the contents are secondary to the package for the purpose of successful saleability. Fat oppression is the clearest example of how society programs our aesthetics. The measure of their success is that we don't even know we're programmed.... Looksism is an infinitely vital psychological weapon of the ruling elite; it manipulates what we spend our time thinking about. If one is worrying about her appearance, she has that much less energy to concentrate on her deprivations and natural survival instincts.[7]

Radical feminists and NAAFA make very different assumptions about the causes and solution of the problem. Radical feminists aim for a more basic transformation of the society while the heterosexual relationships formed in NAAFA are often quite traditional. But both are interested in how fat people experience discrimination not only in employment and public services but also how they are excluded from social life and sexual relationships. Both NAAFA and radical feminists have pointed out the relationship between the self-hatred of fat people and social structures and institutions (for example, the media and the medical profession) that promote or exploit the vulnerabilities of fat women, and both groups recognize a need for consciousness raising as well as political action.

Yet, just as there is something missing in the philosophy of OA and other organizations that treat obesity as a personal problem, so there is something absent in arguments that are made from purely political positions. Although NAAFA members and radical feminists correctly point to oppressive standards of beauty and acceptability in our society as the ultimate source of the problem, they occasionally lack insight into their own self-defeating tendencies and unrealistic expectations.

Consider the argument made in "Fat Dykes Don't Make It," published in *Lesbian Tide*. The author criticizes the lesbian community for being almost as oppressive to fat women as the conventional heterosexual culture. Although she explains that she didn't expect a "ticker-tape parade" when she came out as a lesbian, her outrage with slender lesbians for being reluctant to pick a fat woman as a sexual partner strikes an unrealistic note. Is her lack of sexual relationships merely the product of looksism?

I came out and nobody cared. I didn't exactly expect a ticker-tape parade, but this is ridiculous. I finally got the guts to admit that I love women, wrote an explanatory letter to my mother, announced to my friends that I had done the thing that I spent my life avoiding, and all I got was a couple "Right-On's" and a few cans of diet soda. No one turns on to a fat lesbian. It's not fashionable. . . . Your hot-shot alternative life-styles and "different" aesthetics are lies. Women seem to think of me as a sister-eunuch. I'm not alone in feeling this. Our heads are fine, our bodies do not exist.
    . . . The only coverage *Ms.* magazine ever gave a fat woman was Rosalyn Drexler at Duke University on a rice diet. *Amazon Quarterly* did an interview with a woman who was fat until she came out, then she "got her shit together" and lost weight. The implication is that we can't have our shit together and still be fat. Coming out was seen as the Lesbian Way to Stay Forever Thin.
    I might even be able to find some humor in the situation if it was not so personally oppressive. We have here this wonderful community of politically correct sisters, who all hate looksism and look as tough as they please. Nobody considers wearing make-up or using a depilatory. Facial hair is OK here. Everyone fights a daily battle to overcome ageism, is it that you just need to have your fascism laid out for you? For this I left Philadelphia? I'm tired of people telling me how much they love my head and how they think I'm truly beautiful and then going home with someone else. . . . [8]

Similarly, while most NAAFA members recognize the disadvantages of being fat and don't fool themselves about what NAAFA can and can't do for their lives, some occasionally place full blame on society for their suffering. They have overlooked how their own lack of self-esteem and their willingness to be victimized have also contributed to their difficulties. In a few cases, the stories of pride and the confidence that fat is beautiful gained through NAAFA have a shallow, unconvincing ring.

Ultimately, one cannot thoroughly disentangle personal and political sources of suffering. The two reproduce each other in the course of life experiences. Yet one can more logically make the argument that low self-esteem in fat women follows their shabby treatment rather than precedes it. As several social liberation movements have repeatedly demonstrated, a person who is treated like an inferior or a slave may ultimately develop a self-destructive slave mentality. The solution is to do away with slavery rather than blame the individual for self-destructive behavior. At the same time, the women's movement has also taught us that while we must identify and transform the external forces that injure our lives, so must we look inside ourselves for how we yield to these forces or use them against our own advantage. Taken alone, a political or a psychological explanation and analysis of why fat people suffer seems unconvincing and oversimplified. Only by studying the intricate connection between them can we comprehend why fat people suffer so much.

TWO

*Living With
Oneself
as
a Fat Person*

Introduction

We have begun by concentrating on the fat person's outward life, on her marginal position in a world of "normals." We turn now to the inner life of being fat, to the thoughts and feelings the fat individual has about herself, even when she is alone. For since we are self-conscious and self-reflective beings we have relationships not only with others but also with ourselves. We scrutinize our own actions, give internal explanations of who and what we are, and evaluate ourselves in constant internal dialogue.

Of course, our inner voices, too, speak from the perspective of the social world we live in. Sometimes they represent the view of society and sometimes the view of significant individuals in our lives. The conversations we have with ourselves about how we are doing therefore have much to do with what we think or know the outside world thinks of us, and how we respond to these external views.

The inner life of being fat is best expressed in firsthand accounts, and I have included several. I describe my research methods more fully in the appendix, but to put it briefly, I had long open-ended conversations (over several hours and sometimes several days) with fifty overweight people (mainly women) and several women who are not fat but for whom weight is an important personal concern.

I wasn't very far into these interviews before I noticed the repeated appearance of a few core themes in the women's stories and in their views of the world. First, and most obvious, is the concern that in others' eyes and even in one's own, obesity constitutes a violation of conventional sex roles and even of conventional sexuality. In our society, fat women are viewed as unfeminine, unattractive, masculine, out of the running. In a word, they are desexualized. Yet, in some vague, not fully conscious way, excessive weight is also regarded as an expression of excessive or forbidden sexuality. Thus the fat woman lives with the paradox of heightened sexuality and its negation. To a lesser but increasing extent, sexual interpretations of obesity are applied to men as well. Desexualization can take many forms, but in one of its most extreme expressions the person loses not only her sexual identity but all connection with her body. Most fat persons feel disembodied to some extent—they identify only with their heads or faces, and the head alone becomes the location of the core "self." This notion that fat people are sexually excessive or repressed or in rebellion against conventional sexuality is probably a main reason that fat people arouse such a sense of horror, disapproval, and hostility in others.

Secondly, I have noted that obesity often symbolizes for the overweight a state of disorder: either being out of control involuntarily or purposely relinquishing control. But alongside that theme there is an ironic counterpoint that overeating and obesity may be employed to *control* one's experiences in the world. Just as children often fight with their parents over eating as a way of asserting autonomy, so do many adults use particular eating habits and weight levels as a way of feeling and asserting control in a world that otherwise allows them little sense of personal effectiveness and autonomy. This is common among thin women as well as the overweight.

The final concern is an elaboration of the before-and-after theme encountered earlier: many people, assuming that being fat is responsible for all of their misery, fantasize that everything will change when they lose weight. In fact, this fantasy may be realized to some degree when weight falls away. Many do undergo profound identity changes when they lose (or gain) weight. But more often the problems remain. The theme of before and after reflects a universal fascination with the mutability of the self—with notions of how much it is possible to transform one's self, and how much remains the same. Such deep involvement with the before and after fantasy is part of the appeal of photographs of people who undergo weight changes. The stories and pictures of transformation demonstrate how an individual may be so changed as to be practically unrecognizable; yet part of the draw of these photographs is also (like looking at childhood pictures) identifying what remains constant and fixed.

In the final analysis, the themes reported by fat people are very common, practically universal to the human experience in our society. The belief in one magical thing that keeps us from fulfilling all our potential and that all life would change if this block were eliminated is also found among people who aren't fat. Likewise, the experience of disembodiment is familiar to people of all sizes, and so is the irony of unconsciously controlling life experiences through behavior that superficially seems to represent lack of control.

Many of the themes in the lives of fat people, then, express more general existential concerns. As their stories reveal, what really distinguishes fat people and especially fat women is no unique set of problems, but rather the fact that problems common to human existence often become focused on weight, eating, and physical appearance.

6

Obesity and Desexualization

For women, the association of obesity with asexuality largely stems from the assumption that fat women have chosen not to make their bodies attractive, chosen to be unfeminine, to avoid sexuality and sexual relations. The image of keeping men away with a "wall of fat" is a popular expression of this psychological interpretation of obesity. In this the media offer assistance. Typically the media caricature fat women as loud, clumsy, hostile, aggressive, and undelicate. But the physical bulk of fat women need not have acquired this image. In other societies or historical periods, a fleshy woman has often been viewed as sensual, graceful, sexual, and particularly feminine. The recent four hundredth anniversary of the painter Rubens was the occasion for art critics to note that Western art between about 1500 and 1900 idealized the rotund woman and treated her as opulent and erotic.[1]

Since 1900 our society has progressively regarded fleshiness as unsexy. The reason is complex. In part, being thin is increasingly equated with wealth and "class." Being thin is a kind of inconspicuous consumption that distinguishes the rich at a time when most poor people can more easily afford to be fat than thin. Since idealized sex objects are modeled partly on class-associated images, this is surely a factor. For a man to have a thin woman on his arm is a sign of his own worth, and a woman increases her market value by being slender. Fat women are either accorded a nonsexual status in this system, or else (and less publicly) are granted a degraded "lower-class" kind of animal sexuality.

One discussion at a NAAFA convention was devoted to this issue. One NAAFA member recalled seeing a woman on the street distributing leaflets about obtaining abortions. She described how she was automatically passed over in the distribution of the leaflets, the pamphleteer probably assuming that no man would ever want to sleep with her. Others talked of how they are never approached by saleswomen circulating through department stores with perfume samples, and one woman described the smirks and raised eyebrows that greeted her when she asked a lingerie saleswoman about a stretch bra.

The desexualization process is not restricted to casual encounters on the street. It can go right to the core of the individual. In the autobiography of Diane James we learn of how becoming fat marked the end of the heterosexual period in a woman's life and the beginning of her commitment to feminism and political lesbianism (that is, lesbianism motivated by political convictions rather than an initial physical attraction to other women). As Diane describes, her movement away from men was not thoroughly deliberate but rather a drift, and being fat contributed to the drift by putting her "out of the running" with regard to attracting men as well as by communicating her diminished concern with physical appearance and the conventional values of our society.

In some cases the association of asexuality with obesity is created as much by the individual herself as it is imposed by the outside world. Joan Bauer, the physicist introduced earlier, reflects on this problem:

> My husband, David, is a mathematician. He is a victim in all of this. He has always felt that I'm a beautiful woman. He's always been attracted to me personally and sexually. He doesn't like it that I weigh 250 but he doesn't bother me about it. He'd rather I weighed 170 but mostly he'd rather I didn't hate myself and spend all of my energy agonizing about dieting. He loves me and he'd rather I weighed less than more but it isn't a big deal to him. He's the victim of *my* cutting off sexuality because I feel so unattractive and elephant-like that how could any elephant like me be interested in sex.

He has to put up not only with my being fat but also with my becoming asexual as my way of coping with being fat.

One clue to understanding why obesity is treated as a violation of sex roles is suggested by the popular imagery linking being fat with an autoerotic and/or self-indulgent disposition. Overweight women are suspected of feeding and taking care of themselves, giving pleasure to their own bodies rather than stimulating, pleasing, feeding, and nurturing others. Fat men are correspondingly viewed as passive, vulnerable, soft, and self-indulgent, as if they had failed in a male obligation to be aggressive and achievement oriented. In the stereotype the fat woman substitutes food for sex, she nurtures herself as if she were a baby, she substitutes a private fantasy life for mature engagement with the real world.

If fat women are considered "out of the running" with reference to men, curiously enough, so are fat men. They are treated as withdrawn from the competition between men; it is as though they have joined the world of women. And since men are valued more than women, in the cases of both fat men and women, it is one's position vis-à-vis men that is considered the test of value.

The suspicion associating obesity with an antisocial or self-centered nature is exacerbated by the fact that many fat women prefer to eat in private. They are ashamed and discomfited at how others see them. Thus eating becomes even more a private, secret, forbidden act, symbolizing the individual's withdrawal from the social world and its obligations. One of the most common stories told by fat women is of their furtive visits to the refrigerator at night after everyone else has gone to sleep. The association of obesity with secrecy, darkness, self-gratification, and social withdrawal rather than service to or engagement with others is consistent with the overall image of obesity as a violation of women's social obligations:

> I always thought that people knew that the reason I was fat was because I didn't have a man. Being fat was a clear signal that I was home masturbating with my box of cookies. Being fat was the sign that no one else could gratify me and so I turned to food. (*Ellin*, Autobiography)

In my mind I associated my mother's weight with her cruelty and with being overbearing and non-nurturant and masculine. *(Shirley Kaufman, a clinical psychologist)*

In keeping with the demand that women nurture others rather than themselves, Joan Bauer relates how eating becomes the one thing she can do to replenish herself when she is drained by effort to perform in the traditional female role and in her professional life:

Joan Bauer

Indulgent is a crucial word. I view eating as a safety valve. I go home from here four in the afternoon. I've been carrying tremendous pressure trying to move from student to faculty, trying to be a peer overnight to people who were my authority figures, trying to be everything that everyone wants, to be the first woman this and first woman that, to be the only scientist around here involved in political work against nuclear proliferation, to be the only woman who wants to work part time, to be the student's best friend, the feminist, to do a damn good job in the classroom and get started on new research.

I go home and try to be home enough for my two kids, who need attention, and my husband feels abandoned, and I'm trying to cook dinner—that's when I eat. It's very clear to me that eating is a way of coping with the multiple pressures of a life that feels like it's just got to fly apart at the seams—where if one thing gets out of line it will bring the whole thing tumbling down in a crisis. With that kind of pressure—I feel this is the one place I can be indulgent and I do not make myself exercise control over food. When I need to diet or fast, it's clear that the shifting of control into this realm which is the one place I've always given myself freedom to be—not really psychically but behaviorally—just about drives me up the wall.

I would sometimes stand in my kitchen with tears on my face and I would say, "I can't stand these kids, and if I can't eat right this minute I'm gonna go crazy." And then I eat or have a fight with my husband and say I just can't do any more. I can't be all these things to all these people. I can't do all these things right. I've got to eat. So eating does provide me with the one area where I allow myself to be indulgent and out of control when I'm trying to keep ninety-seven balls in the air. I'm taking care of everyone else and food takes care of me.

The kids are taking out of me, the students are taking out of me, David wants this, my parents want that. I'm trying to be a good neighbor and a good daughter and a good parent and a good wife and a good teacher and a good scholar and a good friend and the one thing that will take care of *me* is food.

Being the one who gives to everyone is a significant part of being a woman. It certainly is the way my mother was. This is the one way I'm continuous with her. Even though my relationship with my husband is different from the relationship between my parents, and David does much more than my father did at home, I still feel like I give, give, give.

I think occasionally that my abilities are apparently so great that, if I were freed of the constraints of this role conflict, what could I do?

For example, I once had an opportunity to do key work on a very exciting research project that had vital importance in my field. It was during a period when David and I were separated and I had one child, and my first feeling was, "I can't do it, and I'm really pissed I can't do it." And then we worked out a way where my parents and David together took care of Mark for six weeks and I was not a mother for those six weeks. He was physically gone. And I worked twenty hours a day, and I was exhilarated, and it was fantastic not to be worried all the time that I was working about whether I ought to be home and whether the kid had an ear infection or whether I ought to be at the PTA meeting and whether I was a bad mother to be gone—all those things that drain inner energy. I just worked like a man would work. Like a super-ambitious, really talented man would work. It was very freeing to be absolutely single-focused. The main experience I have of womanness is to be constantly divided—constantly trying to do the splits across nineteen floating logs on a rapidly moving river and keep myself from falling in the water.

I sometimes have the image in my mind that my husband is like a child and I have *three* children that are always taking from me. I feel like I am the strong, stable earth mother. I am the giver, the nurturer of last resort. If everyone else goes to hell ultimately I am the one, no matter how bad I feel, to give. I will pull myself together and give what needs to be given. No matter what happens—no matter how angry or tired or hurt. As the nurturer you keep on asking about other people's needs and try to respond to them, and you don't just throw in the towel and say, "Okay, someone else take care of me." I'm the one who will keep going, doing what has to be done. If that means suppressing my own needs and feelings, then I will. And that's when I eat.

Obesity in a woman violates conventional sexuality not only through association with self-absorption and autoeroticism but also because largeness equals masculinity. The fat woman may be seen not only as asexual but as androgynous. One woman I spoke with recalled overhearing a child who, confused by her large size, asked her mother "Is that a man or a woman?" The imputation of androgyny has an interesting biological correlate: with extreme weight deviations in either direction, hormones often act to develop secondary sexual characteristics of the opposite sex. Thus one of the most sensitive concerns of very fat women is the fact that they sometimes develop considerable facial hair and cease to menstruate.

One woman who weighed over 300 pounds had developed a full beard and had to shave her face every morning. Only her boyfriend knew this secret, but it contributed to her sense of shame and furtiveness. It is interesting to note that at the low end of the weight spectrum as well, women may stop menstruating and develop body hair in places unusual for women. Fat men correspondingly develop an appearance that is feminine.

At an OA meeting, one man described hitting rock-bottom when a child approached him on the beach and screamed, "Look, Mommy! That man has boobies just like you!" Developing breasts for a man is as devastating as growing a beard for a woman—even worse, since breasts can not be shaved.

In *Grand Obese*, a novel about an enormously fat family, the obese son is attacked and stripped by neighborhood boys who point and jeer at his diminutive genitals. In his terror, his testicles have ascended and his penis has shrunk and retracted into a "dark pink button trembling against the padded mound of sandy hair."[2] However extreme, the example reflects the popular image of the diminished appearance of the fat man's genitals in comparison with his bulk.

The autobiographical account of Diane James that follows touches on many of these themes. Diane talks explicitly about gaining weight as a somewhat intentional choice for autoeroticism and androgyny as well as a way of being disqualified and disqualifying herself from the heterosexual world. Out of the running with men, she undergoes a slow metamorphosis, becomes comfortable being herself, wearing whatever fits, even men's clothes. And yet there is always the residue of her vulnerability. For although she objects to the importance placed on women's physical appearance, she also wants to be looked at and admired.

In fact, Diane James is a startlingly beautiful woman. When I met her for our interview she was working in her garden, a natural, robust figure. She has long, thick, black hair pulled back and worn loosely down her back. Her face is reminiscent of the young Elizabeth Taylor. She has a decidedly voluptuous and sensual rather than an asexual appearance. In view of her striking looks, one can better understand how Diane experienced a confusing split between seeing herself as both beautiful and undesirable. Diane James lives in the Bay Area of San Francisco and is employed by a public agency as a carpenter.

Diane James:
Out of the Running and Glad of It

I'm twenty-eight years old now, and I've always been 25 to 50 pounds overweight. I've always felt that I'm just beyond the fringe of acceptability. My weight is about 170 now but I'm not interested in losing 45 pounds anymore. I'd just like to lose 25 pounds so I can jog, run, and be healthy.

I weighed 150 in high school, and I'd love to weigh that now. To me, being 10 or 15 pounds below a comfortable weight is a heterosexual ideal, but 10 or 15 pounds above that is comfortable in a lesbian situation. I felt good being big when I was in high school, but you're supposed to be smaller in relation to men. Unless you're dating a football player you have to be small.

I wasn't a fat child. I was large and solid, and later I was voluptuous. But then I started to experience social pressures about my role as a woman. I thought I was *big*. I *was* bigger than the boys and rounder than many of the girls. Of course there's some advantage in being fat when you're an adolescent because you mature faster so you're considered sexy.

I grew up in Hollywood, and straight skirts were in fashion when I was in the fifth grade, and I'd be anxious about walking down the corridor in school. You were supposed to have a flat stomach and mine was round, so I'd suck my stomach in all the time as I walked down the corridor. I was terrified someone would notice I was fat or had a round stomach.

I felt good, physically. My fat may indeed have been body armoring, and I accept that idea. But I guess I have needed that. I wanted to look strong, and I didn't want to be attacked. I like the Amazon image. I like big women. But there was no room for an Amazon woman in high school. I wanted to fit in—approval from my girl friends was important, and they were involved in the sex-roles thing.

I was very conservative-looking as a teenager. I wore a long braid, glasses, and oxfords. So through junior high school I was not attractive. I could see I had good bone structure—I had potential. And I liked my looks and the strength of my body, but there was just too much—I was too voluptuous.

People rarely made remarks about my weight because I sent out vibes saying, "Don't mention it." I was verbal and sarcastic. People knew if they made remarks I could retort. My mother was compassionate about my weight. She said it was baby fat and I would lose it. My father did make critical remarks. I didn't really like him so I just sort of flaunted my weight. I didn't go out of my way to win his respect. But I did feel less desirable because I was fat, and I knew I was fat because Los

Angeles is very media-and fashion-conscious, and I just knew.

When I went out on a date I wore two or three girdles—so each one could make up for what the other couldn't do. I wore one girdle that went from my bust to my thighs and another that went from my waist to my ankles (when I wore pants). I put up with any torture I had to, to be within the fringe of acceptability.

When I was dating I felt big and fat. It wasn't just the girdles but also the false eyelashes and make-up and getting rid of the dark hair around my mouth with electrolysis and bleaching. I felt phony and deceptive and armored, with everything held together under the dress with safety pins and garter belts and nylons. I felt physically uncomfortable. I didn't blame the boys for my discomfort, I blamed myself.

When you wear nylons and your thighs are too big, you pop out and rub and irritate your skin. I would be in pain because there were tears in the girdles and I didn't fix them and then my skin would get rubbed and the sweat would pour over it. These things—girdles—rip because you're too big. If you wear two at a time it's especially painful.

I tried to avoid the situation of men seeing the girdles. It was a look-but-don't-touch situation. It was pretty stifling. Some of the guys made comments, like *"What have you got on?"* Now, how are you going to answer that question?

I had one boyfriend, John, for a month when I was around nineteen, and I weighed about 165 then. He was big—six-four—and very handsome. Physically he was a dream, but mentally I could think rings around him. If he hadn't gone to Vietnam I might have had a good heterosexual experience with him. After he left I was in art school and I dated an artist twelve years older than me. He was intellectually and politically more interesting than John, and I expected him to appreciate a voluptuous body because he was an artist. When I did have sex with him—or rather, when he did enter me, to put it bluntly, since it wasn't sexual for me—he said, "Oh, what big thighs you have." I thought to myself, Big? In comparison to what? You know—in comparison to him? I was sort of detached from the situation. I didn't have a lot invested in it—I just didn't want to be a virgin anymore. So I thought, so I have big thighs. It's a fact. But I guess I also sort of cringed at the remark.

I once lost a job as a cocktail waitress because I was too fat. When I first moved to Berkeley I was desperate for a job and applied to be a cocktail waitress at this fancy restaurant. I was 19 but I lied and said I was 21 so I could serve drinks. The waitresses in this restaurant had to wear tiny miniskirts and fancy underwear that was meant to show.

I got this job deceptively. I have farm-woman legs which I like, but they don't go with being a cocktail waitress, and there are 20 women with skinny legs waiting to fill the job. So I wore my long maxi-coat to the job interview—it was a really striking coat. I walked all over L.A. looking for that coat—it was marked down from $250 to $125. And I wore $50 designer boots and heavy makeup, and I had my hair flowing down my back.

I needed money—I was desperate to do anything. Of course, I hated wearing that cocktail waitress outfit. I felt extremely self-conscious—my ass was to the world, for all to see. I tried to be discreet but there was no way with that outfit. I'm sure I still had a short girdle on, to control the midruff bulge.

The job lasted a week—they fired me. They said I didn't serve a woman a cocktail on time—some crap like that, which wasn't true. The hostess took me into the office and she fired me, and I asked her if it was because I was fat and my legs were heavy. I was crying because I felt *so* self-conscious on the job because I got it because I covered myself up and then they hired me and then they had to look at me. You're very vulnerable in a situation like that.

The hostess didn't deny that it was because of my weight. She was real cold. In fact, I think she acknowledged that it was my weight and it was just too painful for me to notice. I was crying and I remember I wrote to my friends about how I felt like a phony who had been discovered.

I've tried to look acceptable, within the fringe, on a number of occasions when I needed the money and had to get a job. I said to myself I may be fat but I have a face that can take makeup. I had straight A s in college, but that didn't matter. It's men who do the hiring and they're interested in appearance. I have tried to make the most of my face in social interactions because I know my body isn't acceptable. So I felt lucky to have my face and my hair.

When I worked as a cocktail waitress I weighed about 155 pounds but in the next year my weight went up to 216—the highest I've ever weighed. I was in art school and I didn't know what to do next.

My whole lifestyle was changing and I was eating more. When I went past 200 pounds I felt asexual—it was a stage when I felt no one would relate to me sexually and it was a safe spot to be in. I don't think I was that depressed during this time. I just felt that I was out of the running—beyond the fringe of acceptability. It was my own definition. I didn't meet any more men. I got involved in my environment, a motorcycle, having my own space. I got involved in politics. I was in a real politicized environment. The war in Vietnam and Cambodia, and then feminist and lesbian politics. There were still different circles to be acceptable to. I continued to wear makeup, and was criticized by lesbians because they thought it was oriented to heterosexual life.

My heterosexual period ended here. I've never been strongly heterosexual—addicted to fucking or catching a man, although I'm sure I've had my moments. *Heterosexual* is an umbrella word; it covers a variety of situations. I just don't like most men—it's unusual for a man to attract my attention. The difference between being heterosexual and more lesbian is that before I was clinging to a heterosexual lifestyle and now it doesn't matter. I don't focus on it. I don't put myself in heterosexual situations. I do carpentry, I work at home or go to feminist-lesbian events. Sexual relations to women isn't primary to me in terms of my sexuality—I masturbate. I'd like going to parties where I could meet nonoffensive men, and I like looking at attractive men who are attracted to me. But it's not my lifestyle. My

primary interest is bonding with women. I can handle
things better with women; it's calmer. With men there's
more adrenaline, more game-playing.

Around the time that I weighed over 200 pounds and I
was involved in feminist and lesbian politics I gradually
started to wear men's clothes, starting with hiking boots
with rubber soles. I liked the idea of being comfortable—
of being able to walk down the street without wobbling
and being able to run away from an attacker or to defend
myself. Shoes make a difference, psychologically. So my
first submergence in men's clothes was with the boots.
My lifestyle has changed so that comfort is primary—no
more girdles, no more binding clothes. I wear overalls
with pockets so I don't have to carry a purse that will get
ripped off. Men's clothes are cheaper and better quality.
The pockets are there for a function. It's refreshing to
remove yourself from being a sex object for a period, or
forever. A fat woman, if she accepts self-mutilation, will
try to mold herself into several girdles. Men probably get
turned on only *if* you wear two girdles. So the lack of
heterosexual opportunities is enforced from the outside as
well as the inside.

I shopped for my first pair of men's overalls in J. C.
Penney with another woman. She was fatter than I was,
and it was like a celebration—breaking barriers and rules.
I felt outrageous in J. C. Penney—I probably wanted to
shock. Going into the men's department and buying
men's clothes was consciousness raising, political,
feminist, revolutionary, breaking barriers, exciting.

Buying the men's shoes and the overalls and flannel
shirts was like going through the ring of fire. I could do
whatever I wanted to do after that. It was only when I
shopped in the men's department and felt free to wear
whatever fit me. *That's* reclaiming your body. I
remember shopping in Los Angeles shopping malls and
going into and out of one boutique after another and there
was nothing I could fit into. Nobody ever thought of
manufacturing for me. If you're fat you're just left out—
cold. So I'm very thankful for the overalls at Penney's
because they've gotten me through some very rough
times and times when I didn't have to think about what I
was going to wear and could think about other things.

I've worked as a carpenter for five years. My lifestyle and employment necessitate these clothes. Being able to have a traditionally male job is liberating. I'm lucky I'm not in a sex-stereotyped female job. If I were back in my waitress job I'd have the same old anxieties about having to act heterosexually. In my job I'm asexual—I'm sure the men assume I'm an active lesbian, whether I am or not, since I'm not involved in catching a man. They respect me too—there's awe and distance; I won't take shit from them. I get hostility but grudging respect too.

I ask myself sometimes if my fat was a body armor against my family, and why do I still have it now when I'm not with them anymore? Looking in the mirror I sometimes look like a rhinoceros or like a muscular man. Visually, being fat does look like an attempt to be bisexual. Or even an attempt to be neuter. And I know when I lose weight I get more sexual, so being fat has kind of an armoring effect.

I was sort of like a clown when I was a fat adolescent. You can have fun being a clown, but there is a lot of hurt and pain along with being unacceptable. Being a clown gives you freedom because it's an asexual role. The clown is asexual, not male or female, stereotypically. The sophisticated, sexy person is always cool; she never acts like a clown.

When I lose weight my body looks more sexual. I get a nice feeling in my rib cage. I can dance better. I'm lighter on my feet and that's energizing sexually and I feel desirable. I feel I look better, acceptable. "Ah-hah," I say, "Some guys are looking at me, so I'm acceptable." Being fat can stop you from doing certain things. You know they mark meat into grades—there's prime, and good, and so on. When you're fat if you were marketing yourself you'd be grade B, so you say to yourself, "No, I can't do this, I can't go on the market until I get myself together."

I didn't go to my tenth-year high-school reunion a couple of months ago because I didn't want to show I was still fat. I think I would have gone otherwise. I think I'd swim more often if I weren't fat.

I have a sneaking suspicion—I'm just wondering—I don't know what would happen if I lost weight. There are

possibilities. I think I might be more attractive to men.
I'd be in the running instead of being in an asexual spot.

There are times when I'm lonely and want men to find
me attractive and times they're so gross, who cares.
When I'm lonely I use strategies like wearing makeup to
look good in order to have interactions—but they're
shallow, not substantial interactions. Lesbians I know feel
put off when I wear makeup—they think I'm being
heterosexual.

Occasionally I try to fit into the fringe of acceptability
again. A fantasy I have is dressing up and looking
elegant and going shopping in San Francisco in nice
shops and being socially acceptable—being thin and
beautiful. But you can't live off that every day.

In a way being fat builds character—it has its positive
sides. You learn to rely on yourself—you don't have
friends available every time you whistle. People are
hostile to you, so you have to develop your own
fortitude. Obviously you're not going to win the first
prize in a beauty contest so you have to develop other
qualities—like compassion.

I know what it feels like to be ugly and I know what
it feels like to be real attractive—the two opposites. I'd
like to be able to stay in the middle. You're self-
conscious when you try to be beautiful and it takes away
from the moment. I hope what I've been through will
help me face the future better.

There's a lot of fantasy involved in being fat. There's
always the fantasy that if you lose weight all your
problems will disappear, as if melting flesh could solve
all problems. When you're fat you're not really living in
the present. The present you isn't really authentic. The
fat person really identifies with her fantasy. You're
always telling yourself, when I lose weight everything
will change. People will really realize who I am and treat
me better. So being fat can stimulate your imagination—
you can preserve your fantasies. So if you want to live
two lives instead of just one, just eat.

And then there's the sensual gratification of eating,
which is sexual in part. Some people have very active so-
called sex lives but they're not getting any pleasure out of
it. A lot of women do that. I feel at least I'm selfishly

enjoying something. So maybe it's a very feminist thing just to take care of your own physical pleasure instead of being thin and taking care of someone else's sexual pleasure. It's selfish but ego-comforting. You can be thin and please your boyfriend and be starved, or you can please yourself.

I can remember on Sunday when I was a child eating a good meal and feeling loved. It all depends on what your fix is. You have to give up some fixes to have others. You can have your steady boyfriend fix—the rush when you get pinned; or you can have the pleasure of being able to comfort yourself.

If I were involved in the heterosexual world I'd be on diet pills, seeing weight doctors, being anxious. This way, I've rejected certain goals but I can fantasize. You don't have to do everything physically. You can fantasize about being beautiful. Usually reality is pretty down to earth and crushing anyway, so fantasy is important.

A lot of thin people are poor comforters of themselves. I think it's good to be able to comfort yourself, even if you get fat in the process. I value comforting more in terms of survival—for where women are now, in this civilization.

Thus the "femininity" requirement affects overweight women. But it is also essential to remember that many thin and average-weight women are deeply affected as well. Many dread the thought of getting fat. Some even *view* themselves as fat when they are not because of their deep anxiety about their desirability as women.

The account that follows comes from a woman who is now of a very slender but unremarkable build. As she explains, when she was young she approached an extreme condition of thinness bordering on anorexia nervosa, an increasingly common syndrome in which young women literally starve themselves into critical illness and even death. In the following story, Lois Cowell retrospectively wonders whether the quest for thinness is not actually a kind of caricature, a self-mockery of the experience of being a woman, since it dramatically demonstrates the physical discomfort, self-denial, and self-sacrifice required in the conventional female role.

Lois Cowell

I grew up in South Africa in a religious Christian family. In South Africa white middle-class women have servants and spend all their time being manicured, permed, and putting on cosmetics.

My mother was very concerned about the way her children looked. At the time I became anorexic I must have felt a lot of conflict between being like my mother—a mother—and having a career. I remember a woman once said to me, "Career women are selfish." I was twenty-seven at the time and not getting married and wanting a career. I wanted to run a boutique.

I had been very thin all my life; in fact, I had tried to gain weight. They used to call me Flea in school. Then I went to London and started to gain weight, and I didn't mind at all. When I returned to South Africa I must have weighed 120 pounds, whereas before I weighed 100 or 110. I never got fat—I never weighed more than 120. But just after I opened my own boutique in South Africa an old boyfriend of mine came into the store and said, "God, you're fat," and so I decided I would go on a diet, and what I did was I stopped eating. I would go all day, working like crazy, and at midnight I would have my first meal—a snack—because I never kept any food in the house so I wouldn't eat. I had a roommate then, so I would eat her food at midnight. If I were starving, I would actually binge and then I'd make myself vomit or take diuretics or laxatives. I used to weigh myself every day and do all this exercise. I'd swim. I'd walk up to the fourth floor where I lived. I'd walk to work up a steep hill instead of taking my car. I went to an exercise gymnasium for an hour every day. I was so thin, 103 pounds, and still I considered myself fat. I reached a point at 103 pounds where I stopped losing weight, but I still considered myself overweight or thought that my thighs were out of proportion. During the winter I would go back to 125 and then I'd starve myself back to 103 again. When I was dieting I would have short black-outs from not eating. I felt myself fat throughout all of this—even when I weighed 103.

I ran a boutique and thin was in—Twiggy was the model. All of my friends and I were competing on diets to see who could lose the most. I stopped menstruating shortly after my first starvation in 1967 and didn't start to menstruate again until 1971. I saw a gynecologist and he told me this sometimes happens when people get so thin.

I was a little afraid that I was going to turn into a man—that I was changing my sex. I would examine my chin and my upper lip for hair.

I didn't realize that I had anorexia nervosa until recently when I was in a class and someone talked about it and I realized this had happened to me. I wrote down my gut reaction to the whole thing. Here it is:

"Ninety percent of those who suffer from anorexia nervosa are women. Why? Anorexia nervosa is a slow and painful form of suicide. It requires such characteristics as self-control, determination, and will-power. It also requires self-hatred and masochism, and women have been trained through all of recorded history to hate themselves. Remember the story of the Garden of Eden... women should be getting pleasure from pain. From fairy stories in childhood, we learn that a woman who is not-beautiful or so passive as to be half dead (like Sleeping Beauty) is to be hated. She is ugly, wicked, evil, and is generally punished for having autonomy and power.

"She is banished from the kingdom, or, fate worse than death, fails to catch a husband, the handsome prince. The process of grooming oneself to please the handsome prince is inevitably painful. Think of eyebrow-plucking, sleeping in curlers, having one's nose fixed. The pain, of course, teaches an important lesson: no price is too great, no process too repulsive, no operation too painful for the woman who would be beautiful. The tolerance of pain and the romanticization of that tolerance begins here, in preadolescence, in socialization. In fact every aspect of our socialization unites to convince us that we are dirty and smelly, *inferior*, and weak, the weaker sex. In a materialist world we are man's property like his cars and ships which are also given the female gender. Therefore a man can do with us as he will. To earn his love we must obey him... and please him. There

the message is that as a female you will never be loved,
wanted, respected, or admired unless you change
yourself, and this process inevitably involves pain.

"In this climate, then, is anorexia nervosa bred—the
condition in which a person participates in her own slow
death. This destructive experience commences innocently
enough. One strips off one's clothes and stands in front
of a mirror to examine whether or not one is overweight.
For a man, this method is probably sensible. For a
woman, however, the criteria cannot be those of health
and strength, for she must inevitably compare the body
she sees in the mirror to those images of women the
media bombards her with. If the time is the 1960s she
must compare herself with Twiggy, and if the 1970s with
Farrah Fawcett-Majors. Therefore, dieting for women
generally has nothing to do with health and strength and
everything to do with appearance. For men, the norms
are flexible.

"Let me recount my own experiences with anorexia
nervosa. I am now aware that I was at that time—about
ten years ago—not trying to kill all of myself but only to
eliminate in myself that large part of me that identified as
woman. For according to Jung we all have both male and
female identities. I developed my male tendencies toward
aggression and ruthlessness and ambition, running a
successful business with male detachment. I was, until
my body became too weak for any sex drive to exist, a
sexual masochist, having sex with men who were my
inferiors and then begging them to hurt and debase me.
Through the use of clothing and cosmetics I made myself
and other women into caricatures of womanhood. As the
owner of a boutique I had the power to do this. I also
rejected my mother, thus rejecting in me the person who
identified with her. Finally I succeeded in killing off the
woman in me and ovulation and menses ceased. . . ."

Like Lois Cowell, the next writer explores the relationship
between her position as a woman and her problems with weight.
In her unpublished memoirs of her compulsive eating, Ellin
recalls how she always blamed being alone and without a man
on being fat, although she now believes that her obesity was
merely a symbol of more complicated problems including the

insecurities most women have about their bodies and her un-satisfied hunger for love. Like Diane James, she is strikingly beautiful and experienced the disparity of having an attractive face and an unattractive body. She is no longer fat.

Ellin
(Excerpts from unpublished autobiography)

I am twenty-nine years old. I am at present about 123 pounds and am five feet four. This is the thinnest I have been since I was fifteen. From about age fifteen to the present I have gone up and down, basically settling in at 165. I don't think I ever went over 170, although there were times when I wouldn't go near a scale. I have never been married; I had one boyfriend for more than a year when I was twenty-one. I never went out much, which I always attributed to being fat. I consider myself a compulsive eater, and even now, in my present state (and I have been on a diet for five months, which is the longest I have ever gone) I have no confidence that I couldn't gain it all back, since I have been on diets before and gained back anywhere from 10 to 30 pounds, depending on how much I lost.

Before adolescence I was normal. My mother has always had a "weight problem," although she has never been really fat. There was always lots of good food in our house, and both my father, my mother, and me had what people call a sweet tooth. Up to the time I was thirteen I was taking ballet and ice skating.

I went to Wellesley College, an all-girls' school. I had never wanted to go there, but my family was very excited that I was going to this prestigious school. All the people there seemed very different from me: they were thin and WASP; I was heavy and Jewish. They smiled and were superficially very anti-intellectual. I was cynical and sarcastic and smart.

My best friend, June, weighed 90 pounds. I realize that she was having the same kinds of feelings about her body that I did about mine, that she thought it was ugly and horrible, and that she probably didn't see me as fat, either because she thought being emaciated was so

terrible or because she just didn't notice what kinds of
figures people had.

Neither of us went out. My experience at mixers had
always been awful. Here I was this fat woman always
wearing black, and all the boys who came out to
Wellesley were looking for those cute blondes in flower
blouses. June and I used to go to the college coffeeshop
every night to listen to the jukebox. We would get
sundaes, and since she could never eat, I would always
end up with two.

I felt really horrible about my weight, but in a way, I
had resigned myself to just eating away.

The summer after sophomore year I spent pretty much
alone in Cambridge. I was going to Harvard summer
school, and I was living in an apartment without a phone.
I had hardly any friends, and I remember my main object
had been to find a man and lose my virginity, but since I
could hardly meet anyone or see anyone, that didn't
happen. In the summer I always felt especially fat and
uncomfortable, and I remember whole series of days that
were like a fog, where I stayed in my apartment eating
and vomiting, reading dirty books and masturbating. I
would emerge feeling all seamy, like I had emerged from
a den. I would wander around Boston feeling like a
horrible slob.

I dropped out of school that fall, not really knowing
why, and moved into an apartment in Boston. Ted
showed up one day and we began to live together. It
was, in the long and short run, a terrible, terrible life
together, but I want to speak about the food thing,
mainly. I got into cooking for him, and this was when I
embarked on my career of being a gourmet cook. Eating
together was the one real pleasure we had. I remember to
my surprise that I didn't feel embarrassed eating in front
of him. We really had fun doing it. (He was incredibly
thin.) And I wasn't really upset or embarrassed about my
body when we were alone or in bed. But on the other
hand, he always made me feel very ashamed when we
went out, which was rarely. He would want me to wear
one of my black dresses, or he would make me feel that
he was ashamed to have this fat girlfriend.

I went back to school in the fall, mainly to get away

from him, and also because there didn't seem to be anything else to do.

The summer after my senior year I went to Europe. It all seemed like a new beginning. For about six weeks before I went I was on a diet and was losing (I was also taking diet pills). In Europe I was getting a lot of attention from men. For the first time in my life I was just picking them up right and left. It seemed like my dream come true. I fell in love in Paris, naturally, and had this affair which lasted for the next two years by mail and by my coming over to see him. I lost a lot of weight (30–35 pounds) and returned looking tan and "fabulous."

Because of not being able to think of what else to do with myself I went to graduate school in Cambridge. I never had a boy friend in graduate school, and this seemed especially horrible, since I no longer had the excuse of not being able to meet men. I still carried on my overseas romance with my French painter, but this was pretty unreal. At least I knew it was unreal at bottom. I gained weight that year and I remember when I went back to see him the next summer being very worried about what he would think. He did make some mention of it, but still said I was beautiful. He used to do the same thing to me as Ted: "I like the way you feel in bed, but I don't like the way you look on the street."

The one pleasant thing about food during this time was becoming a good cook. I used to give dinner parties and cook up very elaborate meals. Somehow eating with other people would mean I wouldn't eat as much, and since they were enjoying the food too it seemed okay for me to be liking it. Of course I would keep a sharp eye on what was being left, knowing I would eat it all myself when they left.

After two years of graduate school I decided to go to New York City and try to make it in the real world. Since I was beginning a new life, I went on a diet and lost maybe 30 pounds.

Well, this was the big one. I bought all kinds of new, chic clothes. My mother was thrilled. Everyone said how good I looked. But somehow, after two months, one day I started eating and I just couldn't stop. I was hysterical, because this time I had really thought this was it, and I had bought all those clothes.

Plus New York. New York is not college, or summer camp, or even graduate school, where if I was fat, at least I was doing well. I was trying to get jobs in the film industry or TV, and here were all these incredibly glamorous young females that I was supposed to compete with. Even employment agencies said I would have a much better chance of getting a job if only I would lose weight. I would lie on my resumes saying I weighed 140 instead of 165. I knew that 140 looked pretty amazing when you were supposed to weigh 115 but I could hardly say I weighed 115! Every time I went for an interview I knew these producers were looking at me and wondering why I was so fat when every other girl they ever saw was a rail. The kinds of clothes I felt I had to wear to make it in New York had no relation to my figure: it was the time of miniskirts, boots, etc. I always felt like I was coming out of everything.

At some point in New York City, after months of unsuccessful career hunting (I was still getting jobs as a secretary with an M.A. from Harvard), I started to work for someone in the underground cinema. The world of the avant garde and artists made it more comfortable for me to be fat in, although I was still freaking out around my weight. I guess people accepted more weird looks and I could get into some image of myself that wasn't so awful because I didn't have to be chic. But I was still without a man, as I have been to this day. And I thought it had something to do with being fat, although now I think it was really about what the fat meant to me.

I moved from the underground movie scene to the radical movement, where there was more for me to do and where there seemed to be less of an emphasis on looks, although most other women in the organization I was in were thinner than I. But there was more flexibility in how you could look. During this time my binging was less frequent. My weight seemed to stay at 165 no matter what I ate. I was cooking less, eating out in restaurants with others, which meant I didn't gorge, but it also was the first time I was willing to eat dessert and fattening food among men as a matter of course. I still went on my nightly trips to the local delicatessen, I still had Sara Lee cakes in the ice box, I was still fat. But I wasn't trying to go on a diet.

What I did begin to develop was a different style of dress: when I started hanging out on the Lower East Side in 1968, there were some other huge, earth-mother-type women, and no one seemed to make a big deal out of their being fat although they were made into "types," that is, earth mothers. I started wearing pants for the first time in my life: I invented for myself, before it even became fashion, the idea of wearing big loose pants with long tunics. I wore lots of jewelry and scarves. I let my hair go frizzy as it does naturally. In short, I looked like a freak. Somehow looking like a freak meant there was a look I could have that wasn't just fat.

Now, I won't say I didn't feel bad about being fat. I felt that I was restricted to looking like a freak. A lot of the times the look in the movement was for women to be informal, with plaid shirts and jeans. I knew I couldn't look like that. I knew I always stood out with my velvet tunics.

As I became aware of women's liberation, I became more and more aware of the way all women felt about their bodies. I remember an incredible discussion with two other women about breasts. Both of them were very freaked out about their breasts: one because she had been flat-chested all her life (she had a boyfriend when she was twenty and had never taken off her shirt for the whole year she had a relationship with him: she told him she had ringworm on her breasts and he couldn't touch them), the other had had an operation when she was nineteen to make her breasts smaller because they were so enormous. The operation had left them scarred and left the nipples all crooked, and she had never shown them to anyone until that afternoon when she took off her blouse for us. When I realized how horrible they felt about their bodies, I began to see that no woman ever felt good about herself no matter what she looked like. A lot of other women tried to help me see the way they saw me: they would say, "I like the way you look. I think you have a lot of stature and presence." I always saw this as a way to make me feel better, and I knew I still felt bad, but I also knew that I didn't feel as bad as I had felt.

I remember, before I moved to Detroit where I was going to live in a commune, hearing that one of the things the commune did was to take showers together in this big shower in the basement. I was terrified at the idea that I would have to get undressed and take a shower. But I found that I was able to start taking my clothes off in front of people and that nothing awful happened. I began to develop a kind of persona about being fat: Big Mama Ellin.

I stopped punishing myself in so many direct ways. While I had been getting fat in my late teens and early twenties I would never go to the beach in the summer, I would wear girdles no matter how hot it was, I would never buy clothes that fit because I was always going to lose weight. I would always wake up thinking I would go on a diet. Over the last few years I stopped wearing girdles, I went to the beach and had a good time, I stopped thinking about dieting, I ate in front of people (to some extent—I still had my private gorges and my sneak candy bars), I bought clothes that I liked and that I thought made me look okay. I had quite a few other friends in the women's movement who were about my size and we had a lot of fun eating together, just like the friends I used to have in high school and college.

I won't say I ever completely relaxed: I still wore the bra I had discovered made me look smaller, even though it had wires and a very complicated way of fastening despite a lot of women in the women's movement going braless. But letting myself off the hook, not constantly trying to diet and control my weight meant I thought about food a lot less, meant I felt less compulsive. I think it was this period of relaxing, of not feeling so bad that made it possible for me to stay on this present diet as well as I have.

These stories convey the pain of feeling like a failure as a woman because one is fat. Yet it is important to remember that for some, like Diane James, being fat also provides protection against dangers and constraints in the female sex role.

It is often observed that to achieve a position of commanding authority and power in situations conventionally reserved for men, a woman must display stereotypically masculine behavior or renounce her claims to "femininity." Some feel, for example, that being fat made it possible for a woman—Sarah Caldwell—to conduct at the Metropolitan Opera. Her bulk made her more like a man in others' eyes and therefore more acceptable to others in a position of power:

> "If she'd been a babe," says one musician, "we'd have walked right over her." Miss Caldwell's success may, in other words, have a great deal to do with her figure. There is something monumental about her. One senses instinctively that this is a formidable creature, one who will prove as immovable and as irresistible as a military tank, one whom it will be extremely dangerous to cross.[3]

For many women, life seems to demand a choice between being successful in love and sex or being successful in work. One woman I interviewed, Claire Stewart, now runs a successful employment counseling agency. She spoke of how being 20 pounds overweight as an adolescent allowed her to escape from some of the constraints of being female:

Claire Stewart

Since they were having financial problems, my father didn't want me to go to college. He wanted my four brothers to go to college but he wanted me to get thin and become an airline stewardess. When my father told me to get thin and become a stewardess I associated being thin with having everything happen the way my parents wanted it, and then my life would be all over. I knew if I were thin I'd be married to a naval officer and have three kids and play bridge all day.

Because I was fat and I wanted to go to college I had to find a way to save money and pay for it myself. So being fat really saved my life because it made it possible for me to become independent.

One thing that saved me during all the years my father told me how unattractive I was was that people told me I was smart and that I had a pretty face. I clung to that. If I had internalized everything my father said, I would have committed suicide. Even though my present reality was not great, I had high hopes. Even now, that's still left over from childhood in my life—I cling to being smart. I never had any doubt that I was bright and I've also always been artistic. When I was twelve years old I made money by selling Christmas decorations I made to stores. When I was nineteen I ran my own gallery.

When you're fat you have your own little world—you have to develop other talents. If I had been thin when I was a teenager and in my early twenties I would never have developed the way I did.

I was in a lot of misery when I was a teenager. I felt I should be a cheerleader but in retrospect the people I associated with because I was unattractive were a lot more important and valuable than the friends I would have had if I were a cheerleader.

I feel completely self-reliant and able to make a good living and talented in many areas. I think being fat allowed me to put off choices I wasn't able to make when I was younger—I feel I had to wait until I was thin to make the right choices about men. I still feel that but I am trying not to because now it's a way of not making the relationships I have really count.

As Claire Stewart suggests, there is a bind—being fat brings both the pain of failing in the conventional female role and protection from some of its dangers and constraints in both work and relationships. Nevertheless, fat women are ultimately at a great disadvantage. Their personal stories tip the balance heavily toward the painful consequences. Even a woman who is remarkably successful in work will have her problems, as Joan Bauer, the physicist, poignantly observes:

I was president of various organizations in high school, including a large social-service organization. When I was elected president they had their formal ceremonial transition of officers at a big dance and I went to be ceremonially inducted, and then I went home right after the ceremony. I had to have a formal gown to go to this damn thing and then go home because I didn't have a date. The ceremony shouldn't have been at a dance— it's stupid that it was, but at the time *I* felt stupid.

We are left, finally, with a paradox. Since obesity is viewed as rebellion or default in conventional notions of femininity, being fat provides women with certain consolations (for example, being able to nurture themselves) and protections (for example, from being tempted to sacrifice work careers for love). But except in rare cases, the failure in the conventional female role is still deeply upsetting to the individual, and like Joan Bauer, many fat women with successful careers remain insecure and miserable:

Well, I have plenty of success in male-associated areas, but I would trade it for being a sexually attractive woman. I'm hooked to the most superficial things and need sexual confirmation in a way that's really sad. A woman who's truly beautiful in men's eyes can walk away from the pain and the ridiculousness of sex-stereotyping in that area much more freely than I can. Someone who is vulnerable in stereotypic roles will cling to them longest because of the forever unsatisfied need to be confirmed. . . . I take all the work success for granted. I've always been good at work. What I'd give my right arm for is to be good at what I'm not good at—at being a sexually attractive woman.

Even in cases of less extreme conflict, the wish to remove oneself from men is usually only partial. By turning the desire not to be in the running into a physical handicap the individual can maintain the belief that she is the rejected rather than the rejector.

Being fat has been a way of insulating me from having to deal with men, and it works. I know that objectively being 20 pounds overweight doesn't matter that much, and I'm probably just as attractive as I'd be if I lost 20 pounds, but it's in my mind—it's a way of punishing myself.

The times I've felt like a fat person had to do with men and my relationship to them—not with food.

And yet, even when I'm fat I still take care of myself in other ways—I still take baths, get haircuts and buy nice clothes. There's a woman who works with me in my office who is not only overweight but has stringy hair and she doesn't take baths. So I stop being sexual to some degree when I am fat, but I don't take it to the extreme. I still take care of myself. It's puzzling to me why I would do all these little things like get a good haircut and wear nice clothes when I stay fat. It's a kind of approach-avoidance to men. *(Claire Stewart)*

If obesity indeed signifies a rebellion against conventional female sex roles, then surely this rebellion is unconscious or conflicted, not fully embraced. Most fat women feel self-hatred, shame, and a sense of failure. If a rebellious element motivates obesity, the woman frequently punishes herself for it with guilt and self-defeat. In rejecting the standards of conventional attractiveness without a clear sense of purpose, fat people make themselves more and not less vulnerable to the judgments of society.

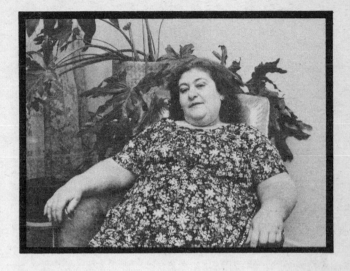

7

Compulsion and Control in Eating

Fat people often describe the experience of overeating or binging as operating in a state of mind where their reflective, conscious, or rational self is not choosing or guiding their actions. Some describe themselves as not truly conscious while they are on a binge. Like alcoholics, it is only on the morning after that they realize what they've done:

> I remember in the summer being eaten alive by bugs when I tried to sleep and discovered the next morning that what had attracted them to me and my bed were the pork chop bones on my empty plate that I had set on the window sill before going to sleep. This discovery horrified me. *(Rose Daniels)*

> I remember whole series of days that were like a fog where I stayed in my apartment eating. *(Ellin)*

> I didn't know where and I didn't know when. *(A member of Overeaters Anonymous)*

> Once I even envision buying something, then I eat it. The decision is made back when I say "wouldn't it be good to have some chocolate cookies?" And I will then function like a robot. I will take myself to the store and then I will eat every one of the cookies sooner or later—

usually sooner. Because I have bought them, I will eat them. It's as though I surrender the power to make choices once the idea has popped into my head.

Sometimes I can catch myself and say, "That's ridiculous. You can throw them away; you can let them sit there and rot." And a few times I've been able to get on top that way. But most of the time a bought cookie is an eaten cookie. *(Joan Bauer)*

Some people describe binging not only as taking place outside of rational consciousness, but, like getting drunk, as being an activity that actually *produces* a state of unconsciousness:

Binges you don't even taste. I pig out to avoid thinking of something else. Binging happens when I have experiences I don't want to remember, feelings I don't want to keep. *(Claire Stewart)*

The same sentiment is frequently expressed in OA when members talk about "anesthetizing" themselves with food to dull the pain and other emotions they can't bear. Sometimes the "unconscious" character of binging is confined specifically to disregarding or denying only that one is eating, rather than being in a more generalized state of nonawareness:

Most of the time I won't even bother to get something I like, partly because I don't want to admit to myself that I'm going to plan to eat. To cook a fantastic gourmet dinner means acknowledging that you're going to plan to eat. I can't do that.

It's because I blot it out that I can eat the whole box of cookies. I always do something else when I'm eating so I won't notice I'm eating. I eat standing up, or I'm reading while I eat. I almost always eat in private rather than with other people. I eat between meals rather than at meals. I eat what's unplanned. All of those are dimensions of hiding it from myself. *(Joan Bauer)*

I would play all sorts of tricks on myself: if I ate things I didn't really like, like peanut butter and jelly sandwiches, then it wasn't so bad. If I ate licorice or jellied candies instead of chocolate, then I was virtuous.

If I ate a different kind of ice cream each time I went to
Brigham's [an ice-cream parlor] then I was being
experimental instead of gluttonous. Some days I would
walk all over Boston, stopping at a different Brigham's.
That way I was testing out all the different places. I
would eat a whole box of Triscuits or Wheat Thins and
feel I was being good because it wasn't cookies. *(Ellin)*

People sometimes characterize overeating as being out of
control, not so much because they are *unaware* of what they're
doing but rather because they are acting in opposition to what
they believe is right, allowable, or desirable. Often the person
feels that by eating she is defying an outside authority. Many
fat people feel that they are *stealing* when they eat. Most have
internalized the command not to eat, so they first "steal" the
food and then ask themselves why:

By now, eating is really like an opponent—an enemy.
I eat even when I don't want to eat. When I'm full or
nauseous. When food is in control of me I binge eat, and
I think it goes back to trying to sneak food as a child
from my mother. That was very much an issue of eating
in privacy, alone, and of how many cookies there were in
the box and her confronting me if any were missing, and
my figuring out how I could get smart enough to sneak
food without my mother noticing anything was missing.
So now I find myself sneaking food when there's no
authority that I'm sneaking it from, and when it's causing
me pain. I feel if food is there, I've got to eat it because
I'm gonna get away with it, and then I try to say to
myself—"But what are you getting away with? Hey, this
is *me*. You don't even want this. Your stomach is sick,
it's full. You're making yourself fat. You're making
yourself depressed. You're gonna be miserable if you eat
it." I say these things to myself, and then I eat it. *(Joan
Bauer)*

It is important to note here the irony that eating is sometimes
used in the spirit of *asserting oneself* against an outside force
or power (and therefore, asserting personal control) at the same
time that eating is recognized as being inconsistent with the

person's own recognition of what is good for herself. That is, eating may be an act of self-assertion and self-preservation against outside forces that are annihilating:

> I sense that the need to binge is a staving off of extremely disintegrating forces. I experience my binging as a means of keeping me here, connected with the earth and my center. When I binge I'm trying to reassert control over my life. I put this food from here to here. From out of this world into me. It's infantile. Binging is out-of-control taking control. Of course it's a perversion and it's out of control itself, but its origins are to reestablish control. *(Rose Daniels)*

Sometimes the individual repeatedly alternates between identifying with the inner voice that tells her to eat and the one that tells her to stop:

> I developed the habit of making myself throw up after I ate. I would buy whole boxes of pastries or candy or cookies or what have you, eat them and then make myself throw up. This would make me feel worse, more disgusting and then I would be ready to eat again. Or I would throw food into the garbage and then have to fish it out. *(Ellin)*

> This summer I was living in the country, and for a while I got into a very sensible routine around eating, and I was also hiking about four miles a day. But I lived right near an old resort town which catered to old Hungarians and Germans and had two or three Hungarian and Viennese bakeries. I always knew they were there, and one rainy afternoon it just got to be too much, going in each day to buy the paper and passing them by. I went into the pastry shop and bought a piece of cheesecake and two or three other kinds of pastries to take home. I remember the first bite of cheesecake: it was so delicious. But then the mania started and I just gobbled it down. Then the chocolate rum ball. Then I felt sick, since I hadn't been eating like that for several months. I threw the rest of the pastries into the garbage. But I

knew they were there, like ghosts haunting me. So I
fished them out of the garbage and then just gobbled the
rest down. *(Ellin)*

Sometimes the tension between the person's wish to eat and
her feeling that it is wrong is resolved in favor of an uncon-
ventional moral position. The argument is stated so that legit-
imacy rests with the desire to eat; it is as though the person
were pleading the rightness of her case, attempting to make
the community understand that *under the circumstances* the
normal rules should not apply. This is the case when Joan
Bauer describes how she has to be the one to "give, give, give"
in a context of tremendous demands and pressure: "A large
part of me says, 'Is it such a big thing to ask to be able to eat
in the midst of all of this?'"

Compulsive overeating must be considered not only in terms
of its meaning as an immediate activity but also in terms of
the functions it serves in the individual's life. Here again, we
can find paradoxes in what being fat does for the individual's
sense of personal control: that is, being fat, like binging, may
simultaneously represent asserting as well as abdicating control. Afraid of asserting herself directly or not being able to
set limits on what others may ask of her, a woman may use
weight as a buffer against outside demands. Instead of saying
no, she lets her fat say it for her.[1]

As Joan Bauer explains, being fat allows her to feel like
a victim who suffers because she is constrained or rejected by
others. She would rather feel like a victim than acknowledge
that she has engineered the situation herself:

I don't know how to handle sexuality—I'm conflicted
about monogamy but I come from such a traditional
family and believe in those traditions. I'm not sure I
wouldn't be as irresponsible about sexuality as I am
about food. One way of handling any fear that I am not
rational about sexuality is to stay fat. So I don't have to
make decisions about sexual opportunities. That is, I
don't have to make decisions *consciously,* because
staying fat is an indirect decision about how to handle
sexuality. It's all related to my discomfort with
nonintellectual things. My family was very intellectual
and asexual. But then instead of coping with sexuality

and physicalness and sensuality which is ridiculous in my family's perspective, I project the "you're ridiculous" onto someone else. I say a person who's fat like me would look ridiculous to other people if they acted sexual. Therefore I have to stop myself because other people would say I look ridiculous. If I flirted with one of those men out there they'd say, "It's ridiculous for someone as fat as her to flirt." I externalize half the conflict instead of balancing the sexual, ridiculous side with my rational, intelligent side.

If I were thin I'd have to struggle with the conflict internally. This way I can just deal with the comfortable, head side of me instead of exploring that it isn't just my fatness that makes me uncomfortable with being flirtatious. I can say *they* did it to me because they'd make fun of me. Instead of saying *I* did it to me and now they'll do it to me. They will serve as the controller of my flirt side. I've externalized the flirt side and put it out of my power. So being fat is one way of closing the door on sexual expression.

There is a flip side to using obesity to feel like the rejected rather than the rejector. Many fat children feel their parents do not love them or would only love them under certain conditions. To assuage this painful feeling, many flaunt their excess weight, convincing themselves that they have personally triggered rejection by *choosing* to be fat. As we shall see in the story of Arlene Bates, even later on in life, women often gain a few pounds to achieve a false sense of control over their husband's lack of sexual interest. The implication is that they could attract their husbands again any time they choose to go on a diet.

The origins of this strategy are usually derived from childhood, when the young girl is injured by not having unconditional love from her parents. The heroine in Margaret Atwood's novel illustrates this process. She flaunts her fatness, as if to say, "It is *I* who reject you, not the other way around":

At this time my mother gave me a clothing allowance, as an incentive to reduce. She thought I should buy clothes that would make me less conspicuous, the dark dresses with tiny polka-dots and vertical stripes favored by designers for the fat. Instead I sought out clothes of a peculiar and offensive hideousness, violently colored, horizontally striped. Some of them I got in maternity shops, others at cut-rate discount stores; I was especially pleased with a red felt skirt; cut in a circle, with a black telephone appliquéd onto it. The brighter the colors, the more rotund the effect, the more certain I was to buy. I wasn't going to let myself be diminished, neutralized by a navy-blue polka-dot sack. Once, when I arrived home in a new lime-green car coat with toggles down the front, flashing like a neon melon, my mother started to cry. She cried hopelessly, passively; she was leaning against the bannister, her whole body slack as if she had no bones. My mother had never cried where I could see her and I was dismayed, but elated too at this evidence of my power, my only power. I had defeated her: I wouldn't ever let her make me over in her image, thin and beautiful.[2]

Yet, as the heroine concedes, her victory over her mother is pyrrhic. She wins at home, but loses in other people's eyes:

I was in the kitchen. I was fifteen, and I'd reached my maximum growth: I was five feet eight and I weighed two hundred forty-five, give or take a few pounds. I no longer attended my mother's dinner parties; she was tired of having a teenaged daughter who looked like a beluga whale and never opened her mouth except to put something into it. I cluttered up her gracious-hostess act. On my side, much as I would have welcomed the chance to embarrass her, strangers were different, they saw my obesity as an unfortunate handicap, like a hump or a club foot, rather than the refutation, the victory it was, and watching myself reflected in their eyes shook my confidence. It was only in relation to my mother that I derived a morose pleasure from my weight; in relation to everyone else, including my father, it made me miserable.[3]

The autobiography of Ellin gives a vivid description of what it is like to be obsessed with food and to alternate between multiple inner voices and their conflicting moral positions:

Ellin: Compulsive Eating

There are two types of overeating I remember from adolescence: one is very pleasurable, the other horrible. The first I did with girlfriends: we would have pajama parties and eat great amounts of potato chips, ice cream, etc. Or we would go out for sundaes, buy pastries, etc. As I began to get fatter in high school, I remember still the fun of indulging with a couple of other girls who were also on the heavy side. We lived in New York City and would go to the wonderful Viennese and German pastry shops in Yorkville and just buy all kinds of cakes and eat them together.

The other type of eating, I feel, was more compulsive. This took place in my stepfather's house. We had Hungarian cooks who would make goulash and homemade strudel and homemade cream puffs with whipped cream and chocolate sauce. My father and my mother would go on trips and describe all the incredible meals they had eaten.

But as I got fatter, there was a lot of talk about my weight. I used to pretend that I was on a diet at the table. My mother would have the cook prepare all these special diet meals for me. Then, at night, after everyone had gone to bed, I would sneak downstairs to eat. I was terrified I would be caught. Of course they knew, of course I knew everyone knew, because here I was eating like a bird at the table and getting fatter by the day. I felt like a thief.

I dieted the summer before I started to go to college at Wellesley. Of course college food is fattening, and once at school I started to gain the weight back. I remember being able to eat at the table with all the other girls, but I was still into sneaking my first year. I hated most of the people on my corridor and I used to steal food from their rooms. I was very scared I would be caught, and I remember hearing people talk about food missing from their rooms, and being terrified that they knew it was me. They probably did think it was me, since I was the fattest person on the hall.

When I say now, "I am a compulsive eater," there's a certain amount of relief. My whole life I associated being a compulsive eater with hiding it. I'm not talking about the times when I ate like a pig with girlfriends, because that never felt really bad. I'm talking about the times when I eat alone, when I sneak food, when I eat so much I can't think that I'll ever stop. I would eat till I got sick, sometimes I would make myself sick, I would wake up feeling sick. But the sicker I felt the more I ate. Even now, when I'm on a diet, I still feel compulsive. I feel guilty eating an extra portion of meat, eating more cottage cheese. Each bite more than a small amount makes me feel hideous, makes me feel that I'm a bite away from stuffing myself. I get an incredible feeling in my stomach: I feel all heavy, like there's a weight or a stone inside it. At the same time my mouth wants more and more food. I feel that the more I eat the more the feeling in my stomach will go away.

Compulsive eating means thinking about food night and day. It means dreaming about the special cake that is sold ten blocks from my apartment. It means going into a store and wanting everything there. But it means never being satisfied. The cake never tastes quite as good as you dreamed it would taste. The little pastries don't ever taste as good as they look. Because I was compulsive, I would eat very fast. I was always afraid someone would catch me, even when I was alone. I would eat so fast I couldn't even get the different tastes in my mouth. The mocha cake would get all mixed up with the rum cake.

I would plot and plot about food. I would think about the different store I was going to go to and what I would get there. I would remember that little piece of leftover cake in the refrigerator and wait until I could get it. To this day I can tell you where every morsel of food is in our house. I know what's in the garbage and whether I can get it out. The location of each new Jack in the Box and Baskin-Robbins is permanently engraved on my mind. This summer when I went camping with friends I was initially on a diet, but then I stopped. So I would always volunteer to do the daily shopping for our food, so I could steal candy bars from the supermarket and eat them before we got back together. I was eating in front

of them in addition, but there were still those extra three
or four candy bars that I would manage to get in before I
came out of the supermarket.

I could talk to you for hours and hours about each
kind of food I like, what it tastes like, where I bought it,
when I first had it. I can remember right now the first
time I had *cannolli* in the North End; I can remember
tasting Italian ice cream in Italy. I can remember an
incredible heavy sweet cream I had on a dessert in a
Middle Eastern restaurant. I can remember meals I
cooked in 1965. I can remember the mint chip ice cream
I ate when I was thirteen. To me the memories of food
are also filled with the memories of being fat, and
knowing even now that it can't ever taste as good as it
really is; but when I isolate it, I think of it as the most
wonderful stuff in the world. And I am furious, outraged,
and insanely angry that I can't have it.

I have always had the feeling that if I finished
everything I bought or cooked, at least it wouldn't be
there any more, and I could have a chance to start the
next day not eating. I have never been able to throw
anything away completely. I always have to eat it all.

I remember the day I finally gave in and stopped at
the Dairy Queen which was about twenty miles from my
house and on the road to where I swam. I felt if I just
got a vanilla cone (large, of course) and not a sundae it
wasn't so bad. But then I got into the ritual of stopping
at the Dairy Queen on my way to and from going
swimming. I was always embarrassed to be stopping for
a Dairy Queen at 9 A.M. (it was also a breakfast place
and so opened early), since who else but a compulsive
like me would be eating ice cream at 9 A.M., but I did it
anyway. One night I virtuously volunteered to drive some
people forty miles to the bus, and they thought how good
of me, but in the back of my mind I knew that I could
stop at the Dairy Queen on the way back to the house
and eat it without anyone else in the house knowing.
Eighty miles round trip for one ice cream cone.

The minute I go on a diet, or the minute I have gone
on diets in the past, each hour becomes an issue of
whether or not I will eat. Every time on a diet that there
is one slip, for me it's all over. If I've been bad enough

to eat one bite or one cookie, then I might as well go
whole hog. At first there is a feeling of relief: yes I'm
going to go off it, goddamn it. But then it's the nausea
and the revulsion. Because it isn't like I've ever really
decided. I've just lost the battle.

Being thin sometimes means that people will only
have me if I control myself. That if I show that I am in
control and not needy they won't be scared away. So I
either have to deny myself food, and prove how good
and controlled I am and lose that way, or I have to meet
my needs myself by stuffing myself because my needs
are too great and consuming for anyone else to deal with.
There seems to be no way out sometimes.

The whole idea of always exercising control infuriates
me. That's the image I hate about dieting and people who
eat in moderation. I hate it as much as I hate the fat and
the disgust. It seems so niggardly and pinched and
puritan.

But being out of control is frightening, and more
frightening because it's so associated with all the shame
and guilt around sex. It makes me so angry to think what
this world has done to women, how ashamed it has made
us of our bodies and our desires. How they have gotten
out of hand precisely because we think we have to
control them all the time.

So far we have been considering how compulsive eating
habits relate to a sense of personal control in overweight
women. But it is essential to understand that women of average
and low weights may also have compulsive eating habits and
obsessions with food. The next account comes from a very
thin woman who has relied all of her life on maintaining a slim
body in order to achieve even a very minimal feeling of being
in control.

Now sixty years old and five feet nine inches tall, Helen
Frank describes the pains she has endured to keep her weight
below 118 pounds. By her own admission, staying slim has
been the central goal, the primary organizing activity, and the
major achievement of Helen Frank's life. Her living room walls
are covered with her paintings. When she was young she had
wanted to become an artist.

Helen Frank:
Being Thin Is the Most Important
Thing in My Life

When I was fourteen I broke my ankle in summer camp and spent the whole summer being wheeled back and forth in a wheelchair. I gained so much weight that by the time I went home I couldn't fit into any of my clothes. I had to wear the largest male counselor's coat to go home.

My parents were dead, and I lived with an uncle and aunt, and my uncle was horrible to me. When I got home from camp he said I looked pregnant. For a month after that I ate nothing but coffee and gum without sugar—I had a friend chew my gum before I did to take the sugar out. Since then I have been on a rigid diet. The only time in my life I wasn't on a diet was when I was pregnant with my two daughters, and so being pregnant was marvelous.

I was very young when I went to college. I weighed about 140 and my belly stuck out—I was so ashamed I used to wear a coat all the time, even in summer. I was so ashamed of my belly I quit college. I got married then and went to art school.

After we moved to Boston my weight went down to 115 and then 109 (I'm five feet nine inches tall). When we lived in Boston, I would weigh myself five times a day, including after every meal because I didn't want to go over 115 pounds. If I went over it made me feel horrible—it was the biggest thing in my whole life. If I wasn't thin it meant my life wasn't working.

In Boston I would wake up at three or three-thirty every morning and do exercises until six-thirty. I'd do 150 sit-ups in various positions—anything to make my stomach flat. I used to eat a quart of vanilla ice milk every night before I went to bed. It was almost all I ate. My husband pleaded with me to cut it out and eat a hamburger instead, but I wouldn't.

I have two daughters; one of them is naturally thin— she weighs the same as I (she's five-nine and weighs 118)—but she has a flat, flat stomach, which I don't—

goddamn it. I'd do anything in the world to have a flat stomach.

My other daughter, Joan, is five-eight and weighs 165, but she's a real athlete and very solid. Still I wish she would weigh 140—she'd be perfect. But she has a successful career, so it doesn't matter so much.

Joan and I are very similar in that we both love to eat. I make wonderful brownies, but I wouldn't eat them. One day I made a batch and went skiing and came back early, and Joan was eating all of them in bed. When I walked in and saw her, her face turned red. I didn't say a word.

When we moved to California my weight went up to 128 and I became very worried, so I stopped eating until it went down to 119 about ten years ago. If I gain two or three pounds I cut out meals and eat only once a day.

My husband would like me to gain a little weight. I weighed 135 when we were married, and he thought that was perfect. I would do almost anything for my husband but my weight comes first and I don't want to weigh over 119. I enjoy living because I keep my weight down.

Even now I do three hours of exercise a day at home and an hour every day in exercise class. It makes me feel good that I do exercises better than some of the twenty-year-olds in the class, even though I'm sixty.

In the winter we ski every weekend—five or six hours a day. When we don't ski we hike—fifty miles during a weekend. We go on scary hikes that I don't enjoy—where it's very rocky. I've had a lot of trouble with my feet—I had a toe taken off one of my feet because it was infected, and the doctor told me I shouldn't hike because I don't have much use from that foot, but we do it anyway.

My diet isn't really good. I eat a lot of sugar, cheese, and fruit. I eat five packages of gum and Life Savers every day because I'm always hungry. For breakfast I eat cottage cheese with cinnamon and a cup of coffee.

For lunch I have half a cantaloupe with cottage cheese or ricotta and coffee. For dinner I have either a hamburger or fish, because of my false teeth, with a little lettuce or a vegetable.

I freeze iced coffee in a tray and eat it during the day

while I watch television.

I never drink anything with a meal because it makes my belly stick out. If I drink coffee in the morning my belly sticks out, and then I'm too ashamed to go to exercise class.

On the street I look at people's profiles to see their bellies, not their faces. I think it's remarkable that a person could come out on the street with a big belly. I couldn't do it. In my exercise class I'm amazed at people who come with big bellies.

I always like clothing that makes my stomach look as flat as possible. When I put on clothes I look in the mirror and if they don't make my stomach look thin I take them off.

In my exercise class everyone kids me and calls me fat Helen. In a way, I know it's neurotic, but I've been quite successful in doing what I wanted to do and that was being thin. It's more important for a woman to be thin. Women are not accepted after fifty. My husband is attractive to a number of women, but no one is attracted to me—actually, looking thin makes you look older.

I was very discouraged when I was going to turn sixty, and I thought, "I haven't done a damn thing in my life. I'm just a dumb old housewife with a lot of art around." But then I thought, well, I've stayed thin and still look good in clothes.

Even when weight and eating rituals are not the central concerns of a person's life, they often play an important role in the individual's sense of autonomy and effectiveness. As the next story suggests, some basically slender women cope with periods of intense anxiety and stress by focusing narrowly on controlling their weight. It should not be surprising that women do this. Ours is a culture of personal responsibility; we are told to captain our own souls and "take responsibility" for our successes and failures. Traditionally, men have been able to demonstrate success through their achievements in work, but it has mainly been through what a woman does with her appearance that she has been able to exhibit her mastery and achievement to others and to herself.

Arlene Bates is a thirty-eight-year-old lawyer who specializes in cases involving women's rights or welfare—for example, problematic divorce or child-custody cases, and cases involving sexual discrimination. She lives in New York City with her second husband, who was born and raised in France. He is a violinist and currently plays in a major orchestra.

Arlene is thin and athletic. About five feet, nine inches tall, she fluctuates in weight between 130 and 138 pounds. She eats large amounts of food, she says, but she burns it off doing vigorous exercise—at least an hour every day. She runs early every morning in Central Park with two neighbors, and she belongs to a gym where she swims at least every other day.

Although Arlene has never actually been fat, weight has played an important part in her life in different ways. She has felt her weight to be bound up with her experience of herself as a sexual person.

Arlene Bates

One of the powerful things I remember about weight from my childhood is that my older sister (who is three years older than I) was quite overweight—she was about 25 pounds overweight in high school. My mother would ridicule and torment her, and call her Fatty or Fatso, under the guise of trying to help her lose weight. I remember once in the guise of "helping" her my mother grabbed my sister's dress and pulled it up and grabbed her thigh and said "look at this ham."

My sister was considered the fat, brilliant slob, and I was considered the dumb, pretty, neat, and social one. When my sister got married to her first husband, who's really a creep, my mother said she should marry him and consider herself lucky because no one else would have her. My sister has never forgiven my mother—she hasn't seen or talked to her for years. She's married now and is thin as a bone, and she's a biochemist.

I think I identified with my sister when we were children, and when I got to high school I thought I was fat too, even though my mother said I wasn't. I was taller than any of my friends (I'm five-nine) so I felt big and awkward and fat. I don't think I was really fat, but I was sort of going crazy toward the end of high school. When I looked in the mirror I thought I saw a huge, fat person. I told my father, who is a psychiatrist about this, and he freaked out about it and ordered me to stop thinking such thoughts.

I hated myself and felt self-destructive, and I think that my body's distortion in my mind was a manifestation of that craziness. The sense of being fat was constantly in my mind—when I bought clothes, how I would stand, how I would always be sucking in my stomach. I was always thinking about how fat I was. My parents defined it as being rebellious.

What was going on during this time was that my parents were forcing me to go to business school rather than be educated to be a lawyer because they said I wasn't clever enough to be a lawyer. And I did go to business school for three years only to go crazy at the end and then start college all over again.

Anyway, after my first year in business school my father got a special visiting job in Europe for a year, and the government would pay for the whole family to go, so they said I could spend a year as a student in France if I didn't complain about having to go to business school.

So I was eighteen years old and in Paris all by myself for most of the year. I first had a room with a French family that was supposed to have had a daughter my age, but she was never around. They had a wonderful French cook, and I was feeling tired and depressed, so I just stayed at home all the time. My weight went up from 130 to 155—this is the only time that I have actually been overweight. Then I moved out and got a little hotel room without any cooking facilities for myself. The only cooking I could do was plug in a pot for hot water—I was supposed to be going out to student restaurants and cafeterias to eat.

But I didn't like going out in the rain and waiting in line at the student cafeterias, so I rarely went out at all. I was totally alone, and I wanted to lose weight, so I just stopped eating, or occasionally I brought an egg or two to my room.

Because of political turmoil the university was shut, so I wasn't even going to classes. I spent all of my time just obsessed with getting thin. Seeing how thin I could get became the major thing in my life—starting in

January and going on until May. I remember I had a belt
that kept needing new notches as I lost weight and finally
it could go around my waist twice and I was so glad. I
liked seeing new vertebrae and ribs sticking out that
hadn't been visible before.

I ended up weighing 115 pounds. One morning I
woke up and the bed was saturated with perspiration and
I could hardly move. I think I was in electrolyte
imbalance and was losing all the water in my body. I
knew I was starving. Also, I stopped having menstrual
periods at this time and didn't get them again for over a
year.

In May when the year was over and I was down to
115 pounds I went to Italy to meet my family. My father
met me at the train station and didn't even recognize me.
He almost died when I said "Dad" to him. He said I
looked like I was in a concentration camp and they
forced me to eat food, which I didn't want.

I stayed thin throughout business school and college
after that—I weighed around 122 and wore a size eight or
ten.

I married my first husband (who is a lawyer) a year
after I graduated college. We were married for only two
years, and I went to law school after we were divorced.

During my first marriage I had a pathological fear
about getting fat. I was actually thin and had a lovely
figure, but I never enjoyed it—I hated my body and
thought it was fat and ugly. I wouldn't even undress in
front of my husband and was neurotic about my body and
sex, and that was one of the reasons he dragged me to a
psychiatrist.

Starting with my divorce I noticed my metabolism
changed when I was in a state of chronic anxiety. It
seemed no matter how much I ate—I could eat enormous
amounts of ice cream and candy and junk every day—I
wouldn't gain weight. I think the anxiety made me very
active physically—I was running and jogging and
exercising all the time. But in my mind I associated
being out of my mind with being able to eat anything I
wanted. I noticed when I stopped being so crazy that I
would gain weight when I eat like that.

Right now I weigh around 132 and my husband,

Claude, teases me and calls me fatso. As a European he's used to much smaller women, and his first wife was extremely thin. Sometimes he'll take the food out of my hand and say, "that's enough fatso."

When I ask him if he really thinks I'm fat he'll say "You're not thin—let's put it that way."

Being fat or feeling fat has played different roles in different times of my life. The dynamics of my thing with Claude about his calling me fatso is related to what's going on in our relationship.

For the last six months he's been much less sexually attracted to me and responsive than he was before. I think the reason for this is that he's been very depressed about an orchestra position he really wanted and it looks like he isn't going to get it.

So I'm feeling stocky and older, and even though I now weigh exactly what I weighed when I met him, I tell myself if I weighed five pounds less he'd be more sexually interested in me. In a way by not losing the weight and thereby having Claude and me define me as fat, I'm colluding with him over his sexual withdrawal and in desexualizing our relationship. That is, the pressure is taken off of him for not being more sexual because I'm defined as nonsexual myself—as "tubby girl" rather than a sexual woman. So he's protected too. It's as if I'm controlling the lack of sex by being fat rather than his controlling it—so I don't feel rejected.

What I mean by being "tubby girl" is that we define me as being fat. So I wear unsexy, cotton flowery underpants instead of sexy underwear. I'm a healthy, wholesome, farm-girl type rather than a sexy woman. I feel more comfortable wearing big, loose tops that go over my hips.

And I wear tubby-girl nightgowns at night—long, ratty flannel nightgowns. Claude hates them. If we were in a more sexual relationship with each other I would think twice about wearing those tubby-girl flannel nightgowns, even though I like them, because I know what a turn-off they are for Claude.

Putting on one of those nightgowns before going to bed is like saying "I'm not gonna bother you and know you won't bother me." But now, since Claude isn't feeling sexual, I feel justified in putting on the nightgown. I like wearing them, and now it's okay to.

I feel loss and strain about our lack of sex, but I also feel relief not having to be a sexual person because that's very hard for me.

On the other hand I want to be admired from afar but I hate men looking at me in the streets and making advances. And I want a sexual relationship with Claude and know it would be more appropriate but if I were five pounds thinner and feeling more sexual I would also feel more vulnerable. I feel comfortable and safe being tubby girl.

I have never felt comfortable being sexy and sexual. I don't like being a sexual object. Claude makes me wear sexy clothes rather than the comfortable ones I like. He made me throw out all my old clothes and said they made me look like a 1950s secretary. I like to wear a bra and he made me stop wearing one—he calls them "tit holders" and ridicules me when I wear them. I don't feel comfortable having my nipples show but I gave in to Claude and now I'm used to it.

In France I was wearing a sheer top and my nipples showed through, and people were looking at me in the street and I felt very uncomfortable.

Claude also makes me buy clothes I consider too revealing. I say, "But Claude, my flesh will show," and he says, "So let it show."

I don't really worry about getting fat now, but I do feel if I lost a few pounds Claude would like it better, although I also know it is a way of colluding to make our relationship comfortable without sex.

If Claude and I broke up now I would probably go on a diet instinctively—not so much to get a new man, but to rejuvenate myself. If I were single again I would want to be very thin. I would construct a new person by being thin—as enigmatic, willowy and mysterious. Losing weight would be a way to defend myself just as being tubby girl now is a way of defending myself.

Before I met Claude, when I was unattached, I joined Weight Watchers in order to lose five pounds. I weighed 140 and wanted to weigh 135. They wouldn't let me in because they said I wasn't overweight at 140 so I had to get a note from a psychiatrist asking them to let me in because it would be important for my peace of mind to lose the five pounds.

When I was younger I used to think I was fat to destroy myself, and now I use it to protect myself. In a way, weight is lurking there all the time as an issue. Whenever something is bothering me or when I want to make a change in my life it seems I turn to weight to somehow symbolize the issue. It makes me feel more in control of things. In certain situations it ameliorates some of the threatening things out there in the world. When the rest of my life is going out of control I always say to myself, there's one thing I *can* control, what I put in my mouth.

Shirley Kaufman, the forty-nine-year-old clinical psychologist introduced earlier has a very successful private practice as a psychoanalytically oriented therapist in Los Angeles. She is five-four and weighs 120. She has been overweight only during two brief periods of her life, but weight is a daily concern, and she feels fat even if her weight rises to 122 pounds. In Chapter 4 Shirley recounted how her mother, widowed young and left poor, controlled her children by stuffing them with foods *she* liked, denying them their own favorites and threatening abandonment if they failed to comply. Here we see how Shirley feels those experiences contribute to her current self-image.

Like Arlene, she explains that food and eating were things she could use to assert herself and to experience personal control in relationship to her mother and to her first husband.

Shirley Kaufman

When I wake up in the morning the first thing I do is put my hand on my stomach to see if it's flat. Then I feel the pelvic bones to see how prominent they are. Then I get up, and first I pee and then I weigh myself.

Once in a while, like after a weekend, my manual check says "Uh-oh, you're up," and I get on the scale and I weigh 122, and then I say to myself "You must really look bloated." Then I say, "No, you're just crazy."

If I'm feeling fat and it's a day when I'm seeing patients, I'll pick loose clothes in which I'll be comfortable and can forget about what I look like. I'll probably wear a skirt with a loose waist rather than pants so I won't have to be conscious of my body.

Except for when I was a small child and for a few years after I had my second child, I have never been fat, but what's bizarre is that even to this day there's a sense in which I sometimes feel fat, and it affects how I feel about myself, how I relate to the world, and my sense of well-being.

One reason I experience myself as not thin is that I was a chubby child—but it goes deeper than that. Saying that it is just that I was a fat child seems oversimple.

It certainly has to do with ways I internalized cultural standards of beauty and my feelings about my mother. At first I thought my mother was the most beautiful woman in the world and by the time I was eight, I thought she was ugly and fat. I've always had a troubled relationship with my mother and by the time I was eight or nine I had systematically set out to root her out of me.

She was chunky and heavy set. The way all those Jewish immigrant mothers of that generation were fat. She was probably always a size 16 or 18 but lied and claimed she was a size 12.

My father died when I was five and my mother never remarried. She worked in a factory and we were fairly poor.

In my mind I associated her weight with her cruelty and with being overbearing and non-nurturant and masculine. I associated her bigness with aggressiveness. She's short, so objectively she's not big, just fat. But from a child's perspective she seemed big and nonmaternal.

The issue of eating was very big in my childhood. There were two things my mother did compulsively: she fed my brother and me compulsively and put us to bed exactly on time. So I would read in bed with a flashlight under my cover and fight with her about food.

My main act of rebellion was my refusal to eat and we struggled until I was seven or eight about it. She would force-feed me and I would vomit. She was a terrible cook—I never liked vegetables until I was an adult because she always overcooked vegetables until they were tasteless and I thought that's how vegetables had to taste.

For a Jewish mohter, refusing to eat and vomiting the food was the way to get to her—it really bothered her. She would always threaten to send us to an orphanage— or tell us she would die and we would have to go to an orphanage.

The big treat in our house was certain kinds of cake. We got desserts on weekends largely because she loved them—Charlotte Russes and something called Mucatars— cakes with whipped cream.

I didn't particularly like whipped cream. I always loved chocolate and she never got us that (since she didn't like it), so I would steal it. By the time I was twelve I was concerned about my weight. Between the ages of twelve and fifteen I'd be careful and fast all day Saturday until the late afternoon and then I would go to the candy store and have a chocolate sundae *without* whipped cream. My mother would be furious that I wouldn't eat her food all day.

I looked like a well-fed, stuffed kid. I knew I was chubby because women in the magazines didn't look like I did. But I slowly lost weight and by the time I was fourteen I don't think I was that chubby anymore.

But I was also unpopular in high school and I blamed my lack of popularity at least partly on being fat because I didn't understand how my personality contributed to it.

I got very peculiar messages from my mother about what was good. There were only two things that brought me approval from my mother—being pretty and being smart. My report card would always get proudly displayed, and as long as she was working I always got a nice new dress at Passover time and in public she would preen over my being her beautiful daughter. I would feel angry because she was never proud of me except as it would reflect on her. It was only when we were out in public that she would praise me. In the privacy of our house she wouldn't give me the time of day. But it made how I looked an extremely important part of who I was.

I was not very popular with boys my age when I was

a teenager. I would have one girlfriend at a time and then get into a fight with her. I didn't get along with my brother, who got a lot more approval from my mother.

After I was sixteen I got a job doing office work and was happy. It was structured, and I got attention from older men and learned how to be flirtatious.

I met my first husband when I was seventeen, and we got married when I was nineteen. I got married simply because someone said, "I love you."

My first husband was obsessed with my weight. I had to be the image of perfection—I couldn't gain even two pounds or he would complain. When I was pregnant twice he found it very unattractive.

After my second pregnancy I was ill and gained twenty pounds and weighed 140 and weighed that for three years, and he never stopped nagging me about it.

If I wanted approval for anything, or if I asked how I looked when I got dressed he would say, "You look fat." Or he would say "I don't see why you want to spend any money for clothes—nothing's going to look good on you anyway."

I think one of the reasons I didn't lose that weight for three years was that I was angry with him. I wanted to be loved despite being fat. Part of my reason for staying fat was that I wasn't very interested in having sex with him and my hope was it would keep him away—it didn't work, but that was my fantasy. I wanted to diminish my feeling that all he wanted from me was sex—that sex was all I was good for. If I wasn't meeting his ideal image and I was still desirable that was a way of saying I was okay.

I wanted to get some sense that this was me. I could be flawed and still be worthy. It was a way of rebelling against his idealized standards of beauty. He would always say, "I love you," but never stopped criticizing me.

I remember he would occasionally grab food from my hand when I was eating something like a cookie. I would just go get another one and not say anything. So staying heavy in that marriage served several purposes. First, it was saying, "This is the worst thing I can do to you, and let's see if you really love me. I don't know if you really love me when I look ideal." It was like my mother only expressing approval when we were in public around public things, and I wanted to be loved for my own sake.

Secondly, I wanted to rebel against that standard of beauty and make a statement about who I was.

There was another thing going on. I had stayed home for a few years after my children were born but now I was starting to do my Ph.D. dissertation and I was also becoming quite adept socially and enlarging my social network. I think this was quite threatening to my husband and staying heavy was a way of giving him something—some vulnerability on my part—some power in relation to me. I was trying to even things up so I wouldn't be too powerful.

And finally, being round meant to me that I could be a mother. It was a way of validating that I was a mother and grown up because, in fact, when my first child was born I was not ready to be a mother. I remember my husband said I looked matronly and I felt offended that he would say that word to me, but also felt it was appropriate that I should look matronly because then I could be a mother.

My second child was a girl, and I was glad, because I needed this child to be a girl so I could redo my childhood. I hadn't been chubby since I was a child so it was a way of being a child again myself as well as embracing motherhood.

I finally lost the weight when I went on a crash diet while my husband was away on a business trip for six weeks. I was able to lose 20 pounds then because I didn't have to see him or face my anger about it.

We got divorced after fifteen years of marriage and I married David three years after that. My weight hasn't fluctuated by more than two pounds for many years.

My pattern of eating is that from Monday to Thursday I'll eat carefully and with restraint. Over the weekends we often eat out at friends' houses a couple of times, so by Monday I don't feel like eating anything but what I call "clean" foods: cottage cheese, eggs, buttermilk, and yogurt. As soon as I start eating my clean foods I feel good—like I'm taking care of myself. During the week I'll be very frugal for breakfast and lunch and then eat a regular but light dinner. But if David is out for dinner I'll take the chance to eat clean foods all day.

When I wake up in the morning feeling thin—when I get dressed and look in the mirror and I can say "Oh, I'm thin," it's like I can just sing inside. This satisfaction even transcends other things that are important to me, like success in my work, in terms of how I feel.

Whether I experience myself as fat or thin is a more lasting high than getting recognition for my work. When I buy clothes the major criterion of whether or not I buy something is if it makes me look fat. I wasn't aware of how much this occupies a place in my mind but it really is a daily preoccupation even though it's not always at an immediately experienced level.

A few weeks ago I had the flu and vomited and was miserable, and the one thing that made it worth it to me was that I was gonna lose a couple of pounds.

8

Obesity and Heightened Sexuality

The paradoxes attendant to being fat are also apparent in the popular imagery of the fat woman's sexuality. Most of the time, overweight women are dealt with as unattractive and asexual, and in time many come to see themselves that way. Yet there is a countertheme that associates fat women with a forbidden, excessive, degraded, or distorted sexuality. The negative character of the sexuality can take different forms. The fat can be viewed as a symptom of unsatisfied needs for love or sex. And since the oral needs appear to be great, perhaps the needs for love and sex are also insatiable. The fat woman falls outside the parameters of ideal sex object in either of two directions—she is regarded as either a mother or a whore. The overweight woman is often viewed as whorish, an easy lay, a suitable target for lewdness and degradation. Or in contrast, her sexuality may have a forbidden quality because she is viewed as maternal and sex with her is too obviously associated with oedipal desires and prohibitions. And finally, the deviant nature of the fat woman's sexual image is occasionally not so much actually negative as simply out of keeping with idealized images of women: for example, when fat women are viewed as lusty, hungry for sex, sexually aggressive, more like men.

This contradiction in being simultaneously asexual and exaggeratedly sexual is reflected in the experiences of women who were overweight as adolescents. The stories of Rose Daniels and Claire Stewart that follow exemplify how a teenage

157

girl who is severely criticized by her father for being fat is also often frightened by his close scrutiny of her body and his sexual intrusiveness. This charged paternal response often sets the pattern for later relationships with men.

Teenaged girls who are on the chubby side often attract the interest of older men other than their fathers, since they frequently look older than their real age. Several women I interviewed first became overweight during puberty, and they often developed breasts and sexually mature bodies earlier than other girls. For many, excess weight came to be associated with frightening, precocious, or shameful sexuality. Several women also expressed the fear that men would attribute to them voracious sexual appetites, as if by indulging the body in one way they might yield in another.

There is another sense in which this exaggerated sexuality is projected onto the fat woman: since she is viewed as a kind of freak because of her size, any sexuality associated with her may take on a deviant and therefore intense character. One woman I interviewed described how she was once approached by a man in the street who asked if she would have sex with him. He told her he had slept with a dwarf and with a cripple, but never with a fat woman.

Fat women often internalize this view of themselves as freakish, and consequently define any sexual interest expressed in them as necessarily perverse or coming from a disturbed man. As several members of NAAFA admitted, before they joined the organization, when men were attracted to them and *liked* them fat, they thought the men must have been perverted, like the type of man who is specifically attracted to women without arms or legs. One NAAFA member argued that sometimes men attracted to fat women seem to be overtly infantile toward the woman, pumping and kneading her breasts like a baby. While there is a parent-child element in all sexual relationships, whether conscious or not, this dynamic plays a larger part in the lives of fat women, or at least is more obvious in their relationships with men.

In Chapter 6 we were introduced to Claire Stewart, an attractive twenty-nine-year-old woman who owns and manages a successful employment-counseling business. Earlier we learned of how she felt that being overweight had protected her from being forced by her father into a job as a stewardess and into an early marriage. Here she reflects on how her weight problems were associated with the sexual intrusiveness of her father and with her subsequent association of attractive men in forbidden oedipal relationships. Like many other overweight women, Claire Stewart has also used her weight to reinforce her feeling of vulnerability to men and her expectation that they will reject her, an expectation that causes her to be suspicious and guarded with them in return:

Claire Stewart

I'm five-five, and my weight has stabilized lately at around 145 to 150 pounds, and I'd like to lose another 15 to 20 pounds. I've been as high as 173 pounds in my adult life. I've been on many diets in my life, but so far none has been completely successful.

I think I was twelve, thirteen, or fourteen when I started to think I was getting overweight, but when I look back at pictures from that time I really looked fine.

When I was a little kid, my father was a hero to me. He was gone a lot because he was the commanding officer on a naval ship. My parents were very attractive and had lots of friends, but it all changed around the time I started gaining weight. My father was passed over for a promotion and forced to retire a year before he would have gotten his pension. He started drinking a lot and went through three unsuccessful jobs in a single year. There were six children to support and my mother went back to school to get her teaching credential. Starting around this time my father began to nag me about my weight—telling me I was ruining my life and my looks and how no one would look at me, how I'd be an old maid. This went on from the time I was thirteen until I moved out at age eighteen. Every time I would put anything in my mouth he would berate me and then apologize two hours later. My mother acknowledged I had a weight problem but didn't think my father handled it right. But she never took my side in front of him.

I think it was a way for him to deal with me being a woman and no longer a kid. I think he was probably attracted to me and he needed to keep talking about how unattractive I was. He used to drink a lot and get especially abusive when he was drunk. I remember once when I was sixteen I was getting ready to go to the beach with my friends. I was in my bedroom with my grandmother, changing into my bathing suit. I was putting on my bathing suit top when my father just opened the door and walked into my room without knocking and made some lewd comment to me about my body. I remember I had poor posture when I was a teenager—it was because I didn't want my breasts to show to him.

He was also embarrassed by me around his men friends because he wanted me to be a hot number. Even now he gets off on it when one of his friends finds me attractive. My first sexual experience was with a man who was a lot older than me. I was seventeen or eighteen. He was twenty-seven or twenty-eight and was a dashing naval officer. I met him through a friend, and at first I had no idea he was attracted to me but he called me and we went to the movies. At first it never occurred to me that the guy was attracted to me, because I didn't think of myself as attractive. He met my father, and my father became enraged and started setting up all these rules like I couldn't go over to the guy's house. I couldn't understand it, because it never occurred to me the guy would be attracted to me.

While I was still at home I just hid my shape, but within two weeks after leaving home to go to college I found that men were pursuing me and I was getting a lot of attention, especially from older men.

I used to eat a lot when I got attention from men; whether their response was positive or negative, as long as it was a confrontation with men, I'd start eating. When I was dieting, as soon as people would compliment me about how I was looking, I would start eating.

Being fat has been a way of insulating me from having to deal with men, and it works. I know that objectively being 20 pounds overweight doesn't matter that much and I'm probably just as attractive as I'd be if I lost 20 pounds, but it's in my mind—it's a way of punishing myself. I've equated being thin with having power. And when I feel like a fat person it has to do with men and my relationship to them—not with food.

I haven't really encountered very much prejudice because I'm overweight, except in a few instances with men. But when men have been critical of my weight I've lost interest in them. I used to work for someone that was always on me about losing weight, and he treated me like an unattractive person. He would discount my femininity and attractiveness by the things he'd say, comment critically on what I was wearing. One time he offered me a trip to Hawaii if I'd lose 20 pounds. I was in my early twenties then and he must have been thirty-five.

I think he was interested in me but couldn't acknowledge it because he was into trim and slim women. Once he came toward me physically and I just pushed him away. He would have kissed me but I couldn't face it head-on even though I'm attracted to him because I think of him as a brother and we're good friends. If I had been thin he would have pursued me, but he didn't because he's socially conscious and wouldn't want a heavy girlfriend. Now he's forty-three, and he's still attracted to young women and has several girlfriends.

When I'm thin I get a lot of male attention. It's hard for me to say no to people, so it's been easier for me to keep myself fat.

For many women who display secondary sexual characteristics early in life and attract their father's sexual interest, there is not only the fear of sexual assault by the father but also the fear of demoting or replacing the mother in the father's eyes, at a time when the mother is still needed. For these women, becoming a failure by getting fat has many reassuring aspects. The story of Rose Daniels, which follows, is another good example of how a woman may make herself into a living monument to her father's oedipal abuse, while denying complicity with his guilt.

Rose Daniels is a dramatic-looking woman in her mid-thirties. Tall, platinum blonde, and close to 300 pounds, she has the appearance of a glittering movie star who has grown very large. As a child Rose was physically abused by her father, and, as in Claire Stewart's case, she was not protected by her mother. Rose also received confirmation of what she had always suspected: that her mother, too, had also been the victim of physical and psychological abuse by Rose's father. A few years ago, Rose arrived on the scene of one of her mother's frequent mental breakdowns and discovered that her mother's back was covered by cigarette burns inflicted by her father.

In Rose Daniels's case, it would seem that her masochistic, devalued mother used her daughter to keep the father involved. Rose conveyed her plight to the world by becoming enormous. As she explains, being fat was, and is, a desperate way to insist that *attention be paid* to what her father did to her. Being fat showed, as opposed to the cigarette burns on her mother's back. It was both an appeal for help and a denial of complicity with her father's sexual advances.

We can speculate that in Rose's acknowledged avoidance of men and sexuality there was an attempt to avoid the fate of her mother. Yet by becoming a wounded-looking person herself, she ironically reproduced in many ways her mother's life experience as a victim. As she concludes, she has used suffering as her main weapon to maneuver other people. More than anything else she has wanted others to know how much she has suffered in her lifetime.

Rose Daniels: Attention Must Be Paid

When I was in my twenties and people would say to me, "You have such a pretty face," I would immediately start to cry, because I was so starved for recognition. Now it just makes me angry.

I'm very feminine, partly as a defense and partly because I'm that way naturally. I don't identify much with the women's movement.

I grew up in a small town in Massachusetts, near Springfield. We were very poor at first, but then my father became very wealthy. I was the oldest of five children, and I have two sisters and two brothers.

My mother says she tried to nurse me when I was born but that I was "too much" for her, and even bit her. I was my mother's first conception and she later told me that while she was pregnant, my father beat her up and then abandoned her in a cabin in the woods, but that she was afraid to tell her family about it because her brothers would have killed my father. Instead, she suffered in silence, an attitude I came to despise.

I was a slender child, but I developed physically extremely early. At the age of eight and a half, I got my first period, to be followed six months later by a fairly regular flow. This was extraordinarily early for menarche, and of course I knew nothing about it and didn't know what was happening to me. But I was walking around in such a daze anyway that it was no surprise that I'd walk around school with blood on the back of my dress and that my teachers noticed it. One of the upper-grade teachers took me to the Nurse's Room, and I was given some Kotex and shown how to put it on. I don't remember being scared. I think what was explained to me was some variant of the view that I was growing up into a woman and this was part of that. I do remember liking that just fine, because growing up meant I could get away from my father.

I was having a lot of trouble with my father—he was always threatening me. When I was eleven we moved from our small house to a large beautiful mansion where I was given my own room. At home, my father began to escalate his assaults on me. He would come home from work and if I happened to be hiding in my room reading, on some pretext or another he would rattle the door and if I wouldn't let him in he would break in and beat me. I hated him but I didn't understand the rest of my family: they treated me as if I deserved it! My mother was never really there—she was like a ghost, completely out of it. Of course my mother didn't buy me Kotex for my period, and my father never gave her any money anyway. I had to get a job babysitting to buy it myself. When I was ten years old I looked fourteen or fifteen. By the time I was thirteen I had built up a thriving babysitting business which brought me enough money to pay for clothes and books and carfare and school lunches. In my father's eyes I was fat and he was bugging me constantly to lose weight. He would wake me up early in the morning and take me to his plant a few miles away and make me get out of the car and walk home in the cold to lose weight. He was always asking me if I had eaten something. I would lie, and then he would slap me.

My binging on food began when I started to babysit in other people's houses when I was nine or ten. I didn't bring food into my home, or my room. Having food in other people's houses seemed like my right. I first earned money babysitting working for my aunt. After she and her husband went out at night and the kids were in bed, I would cook rice, River brand rice, short grain usually, often late into the night. I can still remember that warm, starchy smell that the rice made cooking. The windows would steam up. It took a long time to cook but finally it would be soft and I'd eat the panful with butter and salt and pepper. I remember that it gave me a warm solid feeling inside.

I remember now, too, that I used to imagine that macaroni or rice with butter and warm milk and salt and pepper tasted like the warm goat's milk that Heidi (from the story) drank. I don't know why that comforted me, but it did; I can't remember anything about the story except that she lived in the Alps and drank goat's milk.

When I was a child, I was home as little as possible. My teenage years are a haze; I was busy fighting for my life. I protected my brothers and sisters and became motherly. When I was in high school I got a job as an *au pair* girl for a couple. The man was away during the week—he was a salesman—and his wife was an invalid who slept in a room downstairs. The husband had the master bedroom upstairs, next to the room they gave to me. It was their daughter's room. I began stealing from them: food, and things from the daughter—a pair of slippers, a pink satin ribbon, even though I was being paid thirty dollars a week plus room and board. I had to leave after six months. I think I became afraid that the man would ask me for sex—he reminded me of my father, and even though he was nice I was afraid of him.

After that, during the time I was in high school I weighed about two hundred pounds. I did all right in high school—I had a B or B-plus average, but that was without opening a book. But I was recognized for my writing talent, and I did extremely well on the college-board exams.

After high school I went to Boston University for a

semester. I went, but I was on the edge of something catastrophic. Once I arrived, something very strange happened to me. I was so relieved to be away from my father and to have my room and board paid for a semester, but I guess I was in the middle of a breakdown. One moment I was hysterically vivacious, the next, I was in a daze. I was so spaced out I would "wake up" walking on a street in a strange part of town and not know how I got there or how to get back to the dorm. Weeks went by and I didn't go to classes anymore. I just stayed in bed, reading and eating from the stash of food I had under my bed. I had had periods of "estrangement" before, of seeing myself as if from a great distance, but this was the first time I had it for such an extended period of time. I was able to function, though, because I needed money, and I got a job running the elevator of the old dorm. Why did it happen now, when I had finally gotten away from my father and he couldn't touch me? All I knew was that I had to eat, day and night, or something terrible would happen.

When I went to Boston University I weighed 175 pounds, but I gained 75 pounds in four or five months and I went up to 250. When I ran the elevator I was an entirely different person: hysterically vivacious and talkative. Too vivacious and too talkative. I did sewing for the other students. All my money went for food.

The semester was over and I had to leave the dorm. I didn't have enough money for the second semester. I hadn't even thought of that. I felt as if I were being thrown out of my own home. I felt that nobody cared, and I was right. I was allowed to keep my job at the dormitory on weekends. I remember walking around in a daze with my suitcase and lamp and a shopping bag of food, looking for someplace to stay. I found a house nearby with a sign in the window: Room to Let. I had seventeen dollars. I was completely out of it, but I was able to function. I saw things from a great distance but I knew enough to cross on the green, and knew that it would be nice to have a room before night came so that I could boil water to make my macaroni.

The room cost twelve dollars in advance. I was able

to buy a pound of elbow macaroni and a can of tomato paste for under twenty-five cents, and the room had a hot plate and a sink. At the end of the week, the landlady asked me to leave. I got a job at Jordan Marsh department store and then switched to a job working six to ten at nights filing X rays at Massachusetts General Hospital. I had gotten a new apartment on Charles Street near the hospital. I still had my job at Boston University running the elevator for my former classmates, and I took a shorthand course for six weeks.

I made no friends, I ate constantly, I was badly in debt with my rent payments overdue. I imagined that there was someone out there who "knew" me and what I thought and what I had gone through and he was watching me. I had a special relationship with this "hoped-for" man who would watch out for me, protect me, love me, take care of me, who was always watching me. It gave me comfort to think I was being seen by someone who cared. I knew I was in desperate trouble and I knew I needed help, but I couldn't find it anywhere.

A year and a half after I first got to Boston I got a call from my mother and she told me she had started divorce proceedings against my father and that he wasn't living in the house anymore and I could live in the basement. I left Boston and moved into my mother's house and got a job as a secretary at the Massachusetts state juvenile court. I wanted to start college at the University of Massachusetts in the fall, so I got a second job as a waitress, lying about my age because I was only 19. I also started to hang around with the town's theatre crowd.

Then my parents made up and my father moved back in. For a short while he left me alone but then he started to "wait" for me in the basement. Often he had been drinking and accused me of drinking, and being a whore, even though I was still a virgin.

One night when I got home my father was sitting on my bed, waiting for me, and he accused me of drinking and being a whore. He beat me up, and threw me down the stairs. My arm was broken and my face was black and blue. I went to the juvenile court, where I worked, and one of the female probation officers helped me, taking me to the hospital to have my arm fixed and she helped me find an apartment.

Shortly after this I met a boyfriend and lost my virginity. I had asked Jim to make sure I didn't get pregnant but he was as inexperienced as I and I became pregnant. I broke off with Jim because I didn't love him and moved to New York, working at temporary jobs.

For several months I tried to convince myself that I wasn't pregnant and then it was too late to have an abortion. In one of my jobs I met a man, my boss, Alan, whom I truly fell in love with. Before we became lovers I told him I was pregnant and he offered to be the father. I was very happy for the first time in my life with Alan but I didn't want to keep the baby and I wasn't ready to get married yet, so I gave up my daughter for adoption. A year later we planned to marry in June, and two months before the wedding date I got a call from my mother in Florida. She had heard we were getting married (from my sister) and she begged me to come to Florida where they were vacationing for the winter to tell my father and make up with him and let him give me a wedding. I liked that thought very much, so I agreed to fly to Florida and spend a week with them and then drive back with them to Massachusetts.

When I got there my father was nice to me for a change, taunting my mother instead of me. Things got strained because my father kept wanting to take me out to show me around, the races, the Jai-Alai games, and the local sights and dinner, and leave my mother at home.

My father was constantly criticizing my mother and looking to me for support, which I refused to give him, trying to avert a full reversal of roles. But something bad was brewing—I could tell. The last day I was there my mother wanted to visit her mother who was living in Miami and I wanted to see Grandma myself, but my father wouldn't let her take the car, saying that he wanted to take me to the races. I refused to go with him and suggested to Mother that we rent a car and drive to Miami ourselves—but my mother turned on me with such hatred and anger in her I was surprised out of my wits.

We left the next morning, me sitting in the front seat

of the car between my parents, as requested by my father, instead of sitting comfortably in the back. When we stopped for gasoline my mother saw a telephone booth and said she wanted to call her mother in Miami to say goodbye and did I have change. I handed her my changepurse and she got out of the car. The attendant gave my father his change and my father reached across in front of me and closed my mother's door. He started the car up and drove onto the street. I assumed that he must be going on an errand and that we'd be back afterwards to pick up my mother. But when he turned onto the Sunshine State Parkway I realized that he meant to leave her there, stranded in the phone booth, her purse on the car floor at my feet. I turned to him and asked him, "Do you know what you're doing?" He didn't answer me.

I don't remember saying anything else, in fact, I don't remember anything that happened for the next two days. I know I went into my "estranged" state, where I can seem to be functioning appropriately but where I'm walking around in a daze. I remember looking at the orange groves on the side of the highway and I remember "coming to" at a table in a restaurant in South Carolina. The waitress had just asked my father, "And what will your wife have to drink?" He said, "Iced tea, I think." I know I jumped up and ran out.

Eventually I got back to New York City on my own. I took a bus back and Alan met me in the Port Authority, shaken and concerned. I was in a state of shock, I guess, and after a couple of days, I asked him if he would mind moving out for a while. He stayed with a work associate. He couldn't understand what had happened. Neither could I. I know I couldn't wait until Alan was out of the apartment so I could eat. I ate myself up to 300 pounds in a couple of months. It took me about that long to get rid of Alan for good. I just didn't care anymore. I know I made that real to him. He moved out completely and I lost all contact with him.

It took me several years to get over the "kidnapping." For the next four years, I couldn't hold a job, and I really deteriorated. I know I returned to Massachusetts, then went to California, lost a lot of weight (150 pounds), went back to Florida to show my parents, went up to Cape Cod, to do waitress work for the season so I could have enough money to go back to school, but instead ate myself up to 300 pounds again. Eventually I returned to Massachusetts and got an apartment in Amherst. I was twenty-seven, and four years of my life had just gone by without my knowing it. I returned finally to the University of Massachusetts for two years and finished my college work at long last when I was thirty-two years old. At first I had been very withdrawn, had no friends and no life. I weighed 327 pounds and had trouble getting uniforms for my waitress jobs. But I was befriended by a teacher who saved my life. She got money from my father for me to go into therapy and she drew me up and helped me.

During the period from 1963 to 1972 I had no sexual relations. I may have had sex three or four times in the whole eight years.

I am very concerned with my psychology and how to lead a good life. Overeating is a problem, it's not natural. Animals don't overeat unless something is wrong. It's a symptom. I was in a therapy group and the therapist said, "Finish the statement: The good thing about being fat is...." I said the good thing about being fat is that it's obvious there is something wrong. It's a statement that something was wrong with my childhood, with the way my father treated me. There is absolutely no way to hide 300 pounds.

Being fat hurts me physically. I have labile hypertension. My blood pressure fluctuates between normal and abnormally high. I've had angina pectoris several times, and I think it might be related to overeating and a broken heart. I'm hypochondriachal, but I don't want to know if I'm really hurting my body because I'm not ready to lose weight. If I've had a heart attack all the doctor can do is tell me to lose weight and I already know I have to do that. I had a polyp removed from my cervix three or four years ago and I haven't had a pap smear since because if I have cancer, I don't want to have my uterus removed.

There are times when I need to know I'll have food. If I don't know it I feel insecure. When I go berserk I leave the world and go into a hole with macaroni. If I'm going out with other people and I'm not in control of the food, I don't trust my friends to make sure that food will be provided. For example, the first time my writer's group met I knew we were going to be fed but I didn't know what it would be like. I was at the mercy of a bus trip to New Jersey, so I brought along apples and cheese. As it turned out, there was a feast, but I had to be sure I brought food along.

I will eat before I go to a party. Other people drink before they go to a party, but I eat so I won't want food at the party. I don't want to be stranded somewhere without access to food. I've been without nourishment in my life, and I need to know there will be food. I eat a fairly healthy diet, good food, but a great deal of it. I eat three thousand calories a day instead of two thousand. Usually good food, except when I'm binging on spaghetti and butter.

I've been fat so long that it's hard for me to differentiate what being fat has done to my life. It's hurt me because people don't take me seriously. I'm very intelligent and I have a college degree, but I'm a typist. I haven't been able to make a dent in the world. If I had been thinner I could have gone further. People are surprised when they find out I'm smart. It's hard for me to get a job, even as a secretary. When I applied for my present job as a typist in a hospital, I was turned down at first because I was told the insurance coverage wouldn't accept me. So I took a job as a temporary secretary in the hospital and showed them how efficient I am and then they hired me on a regular basis. I haven't been able to live up to my potential.

My life would also be fuller if I had better relationships with men. If I were thinner I'd be more attractive to men and I think I would feel better about myself. At 300 pounds I consider myself in the freak class. If I weighed two hundred pounds I would consider myself in the range of normal.

Being fat also stopped me from being a therapist. I went to California for training to become a therapist in bioenergetics. When I had first met the therapist who was running the school I weighed around 225 or 230, but by the time I got to California I weighed 300. He didn't say anything about my weight at first, but then in one of my group classes with him he said to me "If you would lose some weight I would like to fuck you." I went berserk. I had been flattered by his interests until then, but this really upset me. Every time my life gets screwed up it's when some man takes power and control and manipulates me, and I let him. I tried to get the therapist to talk about how he had upset me in front of the group but he denied he had ever said it and said he wouldn't let me into the program until I worked on my paranoia and my weight.

I've had to deal with a lot of hurtful situations but I try to hold on to the thought that I'm not bad—that my father was, but I'm not. So people don't get my sanction for hurting me. I remember once I was in California. I weighed around 225 and I was wearing a black bathing suit on the beach and some rotten teenagers came and settled a few yards away. The beach was empty except for me and them. They started throwing stones and shells at me and called me names, because I was fat. There were three boys and three girls. I walked over to them and confronted them and said "I want you to know how much I have suffered in my lifetime." I used my suffering as a weapon to maneuver them. I knew they had never been confronted. I was standing tall and felt right. They got up and left. It was partly an act, because I was more angry than suffering.

Once on the Fifth Avenue bus I was sitting in the back and some little boys in school uniforms got on. Two of the boys were poking each other and giggling and devising a scheme that had to do with me. Then one of them came over to me and said, "Lady, my father works for Ripley's Believe It Or Not," as a comment on my weight. I said to him, "I'm not afraid to hurt little boys that are tinier than I when they hurt me." And they ran away.

I've never held with my therapists who said that I ate in order to be fat so that my father would reject me, and men now would reject me and I wouldn't have to deal with my sexual feelings. That was never the purpose of my eating. I may very well have made good use of the results of my overeating but the purpose was immediate, not long range. I could not have held to such a long-range plan long enough to carry it out. I needed results immediately, not months later. I've always felt that it's tragic that overeating has made me so fat because I think being grossly overweight has kept people from helping me when they otherwise might have.

When I was younger I was very reckless—the feeling I remember is maybe something would go wrong and they'd find out about my father. I've wanted to be out from under this man all my life and I'm still fighting the battle. The result of my binging is that I weigh three hundred pounds and that tells people that something is wrong. That attention must be paid.

For some women, obesity is consciously associated with oedipal taboos and forbidden sexuality not so much because they remember being frightened by their father's interest as that they remember worrying about losing their mothers, or being punished by jealous mothers.

Judy Katz, a thirty-five-year-old psychiatric social worker, described the sexual rivalry her mother inflicted on her, a competition which her mother had to be sure to win. Yet her mother berated her for being fat at the same time that she encouraged it. When she was in the third grade, her mother costumed her as a pig for a masquerade party. Judy's mother also refused to make mother-daughter outfits for them, because she claimed she did not want others to draw comparisons between them since it was inappropriate that a mother should look better than a daughter. At large family gatherings, Judy's mother made her try on potential hand-me-down clothes from older cousins, even though it should have been obvious that they weren't going to fit and that Judy would be humiliated in front of all the relatives. Judy hated being fat, but she was afraid of the alternative: "When I was twelve my mother said to me, 'My turn is over—it's your turn now.' I thought if I became pretty my mother would die, so I made a decision not to enter the competition."

In other cases, women use obesity not only to express how they have been victimized by their mothers or fathers in the past but to make themselves victims of men in the present. Rejection by men has become a motivating force in their lives. In many of these cases, the dominant childhood experience was a father's withdrawal and rejection rather than his sexual intrusiveness. Because the oedipal experience is so strongly colored by the father's absence or his inability to love his daughter, in later life the woman may eroticize rejection. By eroticizing rejection I mean that she is most likely to fall in love with men who will reject or leave her. Love, for this kind of woman, is always characterized by her intense and unsuccessful attempts to please, and the man's inevitable withholding of love and approval. Her early experience with her father is repeated.

In her autobiography, Ellin informs us that her father committed suicide when she was eleven years old. Her complicated relationships with diet doctors suggest that this massive rejection by her father contributed to a fixation on hunger and eating as a displacement of her unfulfilled need for love from men. In her story, it is only the painful rejection by the hypnotist that motivates her to accomplish what she strives for. Although Ellin fears that other people will view her obesity as a substitute for *sexuality*, there is probably wisdom in the words of her family doctor who tells her that she eats out of hunger for *love*.

Ellin

I always thought that people knew that the reason I was fat was because I didn't have a man. Being fat was a clear signal that I was home masturbating with my box of cookies. Being fat was the sign that no one else could gratify me, and so I turned to food.

Being fat was the sign that I had uncontrollable sexual desires. I remember seeing 8½ and realizing how the huge fat woman in his childhood stood for sex and disgusting sex. That was what I felt I stood for.

At the same time that I felt being fat made me less sexually attractive to men, it also backfired. Because I also realized that any men who found me attractive, found me attractive in terms of being a big sex symbol, earth mother, voluptuous, etc. When I was about sixteen or seventeen I stood out from the other girls in high school by looking like a woman, not a teenager. I felt that I had to act really sexy because that was the only thing I could be.

But I felt my sexuality was grotesque. It was coming out all over the place. People used to stop me on the street and ask me, "How much?" I thought I looked like a whore (evidently I did, since some men treated me like that). In New York City, where everyone gets yelled at on the streets, it was especially horrifying for me, since people would say, "Hey, big tits," or pinch me or something.

When I was twelve or thirteen I was thin and flat chested. I was horrified that I had no breasts and that I hadn't gotten my period. I used to stuff cotton into my bra, but I knew everyone could tell that I did it. At summer camp I had to go through enormous rituals of dressing in secret so I could get the cotton in. I remember once someone asking me if I stuffed my bra and being mortified and saying no. I think now that maybe one of the reasons, among many, that I began to eat was to get more sexy. Well, I certainly overcompensated.

But I felt I had no choice. Either I was sexually unattractive because I was fat, or I was the biggest sex symbol going. So either people were going to treat me as though I had no sexual appeal for them or they were going to treat me as though I was nothing else. I felt that if I was going to be this huge earth-mother type, then I couldn't be uptight about sex, which I was for a long time. Nothing about my body made any sense except that it was disgusting and told everyone that I was disgusting.

Being fat meant that I had uncontrollable desires, that I was voracious. It was a clear danger sign to men: stay away, this woman will eat you up. Somehow it seemed worse for women to have these desires, and I think it's something that we get told all the time. Appetite equals sexual appetite; having a sundae is letting go. Eating someone equals going down on them. I felt my eating all that cake and ice cream meant I wasn't getting sex, and look how much sex I must need if I had to eat so much to compensate. Since I couldn't control myself around food I wouldn't be able to control myself around men; since no food ever satisfied me, no man ever would.

I thought if I ever came on to any man that it would seem especially disgusting because I was fat. If I was fat

I had no right to expect that anyone would want me, so how absurd and pathetic and disgusting for me to be flirting. I thought I should act as though I never expected anyone to look at me sexually, yet at the same time I felt I was displaying my sexuality for all the world to see. And it was disgusting.

I felt shame all my life around my compulsive eating. I felt it was like masturbating. Sometimes I feel like my vagina is another mouth, that it wants to eat, too, and if I stuff my mouth maybe that feeling will go away. Compulsive eating makes me feel like a big baby who's out of control. Grownups don't stuff themselves with cakes and candy.

Everyone knows my secret, everyone knows my shame. I feel hideous if I eat an ice cream cone on the street: everyone is saying, "What's that fat slob doing eating an ice cream cone?"

When I first went on diets in my late teens just before college and in my first summer after college I went to a very kindly doctor who was fat himself. He would hug me and tell me I just needed a father to love me. Of course that fit in with what I was thinking, and so I did stay on diets when I went to him. At least for a while. He never really made me feel guilty or got angry at me, and neither did another older doctor that I went to for about a week one summer in Cambridge. This first doctor gave me thyroid pills and diet pills. The second diet he put me on was also some incredible starvation routine of about five hundred calories. The second doctor put me on one of those balanced diets and didn't want to see me for two weeks. I managed to lose 10 pounds in those two weeks by eating sensibly one or two days, then eating compulsively and forcing myself to throw up. But I was so freaked by the fact that I lost the 10 pounds anyway and that he wasn't mad when I confessed to eating all the pastries, that I just didn't go back.

Ironically, the doctor who gave me the best diet and the one I'm on now, the one I stuck to first for two months, was the most terrifying to me. The first thing he said was that he couldn't help me because I was a compulsive eater and compulsive eaters always failed. I started to cry in the office, saying I came here, I've gone through all these tests, please, please I want to lose weight. So then he relented. But even when I stuck to the diet, and I wrote down religiously every morsel of food I had put in my mouth he was always saying, "You're not losing enough." The women who worked in his office were incredibly thin, and they would do a urine test each week to check if you were eating any sugar. I was always ashamed of myself in front of them and always figured I was his least successful patient. Even now I still want to prove myself to him, and I think constantly about going back to New York for an appointment. I somehow think, even though I know that I have lost all this weight by myself, that he will tell me something to reassure me. And a few weeks ago I did call him because I began to fixate on whether or not I could eat sardines (I have been eating them and I have lost the weight). Somehow I can't believe that there isn't some magic word that he can tell me that will make me feel better. And it did make me feel better to talk to him!

This fall I went to a hypnotist when I just started the diet. I had an appointment for 8 A.M., and I had called the afternoon before just to check on the time. When I got there I had to wait an hour. So naturally I was pretty angry. I pointed out that they had mixed up the appointment, and in this soothing voice he kept on saying no, it was my mistake. The office had all this music and he had one of those neat little beards and looked just like someone trying to be hip and understanding. I knew I couldn't stand him right from the start, but I couldn't leave. When I got angry about the appointment mix-up and said, at least they should just admit their mistake and not keep acting like I was crazy, he said, "I don't think this will work out at all." Now I knew I wasn't going to be able to stand him, but the minute he said that I had to prove that I could be a good patient.

We then started talking in his office and I was telling him the diet I was on. He kept on finding fault with it. I kept on saying, "Look, I've been on diets for fifteen years now, I know what to eat. I don't need you to tell me how to eat, I need you to hypnotize me." He kept on saying, "You've never been successful, you've never been a successful dieter. You have a very aggressive personality; you didn't come in here asking me for help; you came in here telling me what I could do for you." And I sat for an hour taking all this abuse and feeling like the worst person in the world because this hypnotist didn't like me. It took me all day to get over that appointment, and I was terrified that he was right.

Men who are drawn to very fat women often see them as either mothers or whores. Of course, mother and whore elements are present in many men's conscious and unconscious fantasies about the sexuality of women, whatever their size. But these associations often seem more explicit, more exaggerated, or simply closer to the surface in fantasies involving very fat women.

The association of largeness or fleshiness with the mother is self-explanatory. Being with a very large woman can invoke memories of one's smallness in comparison with the mother's towering body. Sometimes the weight of the woman gives her the character of an infirm, dependent parent. Frequently men are very solicitous about the fat woman's physical comfort. For example, departing from a NAAFA dance, one experienced fat admirer could be overheard reassuring his partner: "We'll walk slowly to Sixth Avenue and take a cab home," displaying the consideration for physical vulnerability usually reserved for an elder. In this example, the man seems to take the part of the good, thoughtful, son. But before the same dance, another large NAAFA member complained with resignation of her boyfriend's attitude as one of a provocative, difficult son: "He'll flirt with other women at the dance and he'd prefer me to be there and watch it because then he'll be like a naughty boy in front of his mother." Clearly, the fat woman may be motherly because she is the figure one proves one's goodness to, or alternatively because she will patiently stand by and endure one's badness.

The dark side of the fat woman's image is of the whore, of the woman as an object that does not demand or require respect. The idea ties in, of course, with her presumed sexual hunger and desperation, discussed earlier, and her eagerness to please and be of service. This is part of the turn-on for the man.

For some men, the fat woman seems more "durable" and less fragile than the slender one. With such a woman these men feel they can "let themselves go" and have a kind of uninhibited sexual enjoyment that is not possible with a woman who is idealized and fragile. One man who was not drawn solely to fat women but who could identify with the attraction explained to me that a fat woman, viewed as either maternal or degradable, is "serviceable": "they can withstand you—you don't have to hold back. You can really put it to them. You feel you can penetrate deeper and fuck longer with them because they are big and strong, more like equals. The idealized female has to be treated gingerly, you have to be careful. The fat woman is like a hooker, you can let it all hang out." But as this speaker added, after a man has let it all hang out with a woman, he doesn't want to stay around with her: "You can't idealize and love a woman who's seen you in your violence. Once you've revealed your own fantasies and weaknesses you want to run from them. These women know you in your worst possible way."

If in our culture fat women come to symbolize either the mother (with whom men can be weak, demanding, dependent, infantile) or the whore (with whom men can be abusive or violently sexual without obligation or guilt), they are also the worst victims of our sex-role typing. For since they represent what is split off from the image of the ideal woman they are given none of the privileges of being a desirable woman and are also narrowly exposed to what is felt to be the worst sides of men—indeed, to what is split off from the "ideal" man.

One might well ask why fat women tolerate such abuse. For many it is because they have no choice—they feel they must take this or nothing. And for some, this sadistic treatment is felt to be deserved. Since some of the women feel guilty about their own sexuality (whether because of their precocious development and too successfully replacing their mothers or because they have learned to eroticize rejection by men because their own fathers were absent, unloving or withdrawn) the poor treatment they receive from men seems consistent with their own shame and self-hatred.

But the willingness to be a victim is not simply a product of childhood traumas and individual neurosis. These dynamics, however much they fulfill individual needs, flourish in a social context that worships the notion of an "ideal" man or woman. So many women victimize themselves by devaluing their own bodies because our culture systematically produces feelings of worthlessness and shame in women and sadism, inadequacy, and guilt in men. If being fat fulfills "masochistic" needs in some women, it is a masochism that is widely produced in our society and clearly is not restricted to overweight women.

9

The Disembodiment
of the Self: Splitting the Body
from the Mind

One day, while I was sitting up in bed, leafing through
one of my father's detective novels, I happened to glance
down at my body. I'd thrown the bedcovers off, as it was
warm, and my nightgown had ridden up. I didn't usually
look at my body, in a mirror or in any other way; I snuck
glances at parts of it now and then, but the whole thing
was too overwhelming. There, staring me in the face,
was my thigh. It was enormous, it was gross, it was like
a diseased limb, the kind you see in pictures of jungle
natives; it spread on forever, like a prairie photographed
from a plane, the flesh not green but bluish-white, with
veins meandering across it like rivers. It was the size of
three ordinary thighs. I thought, That is really my thigh.
It really is, and then I thought, this can't possibly go
on.[1]

One of the most common adaptations to being fat is to
disembody one's self—to live only in one's head. Fat people
often think of themselves solely in terms of the "neck up."
Their bodies are disowned, alienated, foreign, perhaps stub-
bornly present but not truly a part of the real self. The body
is regarded as an unwanted appendage of the head-self; the
head tries to distance and dissociate itself from the body as
much as possible. The alienation of the fat body from the self
is reflected in the aphorism, "Trapped inside every fat person

is a thin person trying to get out." The body is a source of pleasure only in the act of doing the very thing, eating, that creates the alienation:

> I feel so terrible about the way I look that I cut off connection with my body. I operate from the neck up. I do not look in mirrors. I do not want to spend time buying clothes. I do not want to spend time with make-up because it is painful for me to look at myself. I do look at my face when I have to, to comb my hair, and use only a mirror that will reveal just my face. I have receded from the physical world. I've receded from exercise. I feel bodily uncomfortable. I block out sexuality. I block out food. I block out the feeling of my body being used, looked at, put to work, employed, any of those things—adorned, dressed. I eat as a way of communicating between my mind and my body. It's as though food says, "Hello down there!" *(Joan Bauer)*

The degree of disembodiment varies. In some cases the individual doesn't so much deny the existence of her body as she tries to distract attention from it, characteristically using her head:

> Fat people are always telling stories and smiling a lot because they want to distract people's attention away from their bodies. *(A filmmaker)*

When a person is fat, she feels most vulnerable about being seen from behind. Indeed she is reluctant even to look at her own back because her face-self is not there to dominate the situation:

> When I teach a class I hate to turn my back when I write on the blackboard. It's easier to stand up in front of the class when I'm facing them. *(A high-school teacher)*

> I hated shopping and looking at myself in three-way mirrors because I would have to see what my body looked like from the back, without my face there to distract from it. *(A graduate student of English literature)*

Wherever possible, the fat person tries to build a life around her head. She may even try to construct relationships that make the least of her body. For example, one woman wrote to *Weight Watchers* magazine[2] with the following problem. She was lonely, thirty-five years old and pretty, but she weighed 234 pounds. She worked as a night-shift operator for a telephone-answering service. One of her clients was a man who, also a nightworker, would call at three in the morning for his messages and have long conversations with her because no one else he knew was awake at that hour. They became friends over the telephone and finally he expressed an interest in meeting her in person. The woman was distraught because she had told him everything about herself but her weight and feared she would lose his friendship once he saw her body.

The expression *"such a pretty face"* has been directed at almost every overweight woman I interviewed, and to some extent each has built an identity around the hope and tragedy implicit in that phrase. But what is it about the face that allows people to so completely lodge their identities within it?

Some insight is offered by the philosopher and sociologist Georg Simmel, who wrote about the aesthetic significance of the face. Simmel was primarily interested in the intrinsic qualities of the face that account for its importance as a subject of art, but the same points can be made about its importance to social interactions.

Simmel argued that the essential accomplishment of the mind (and of the life process itself) is to transform the multiple and dynamic elements of the world into a unity or series of unities. Of all the parts of the body, the face possesses the highest degree of synthesis and unity. That is why the slightest change of any facial element (for example a curl of the lips, a frown) transforms the entire expression.

Its special position on the body adds to the face's self-sufficient character:

> The unity of the face is accentuated by the head's resting on the neck, which gives the head a sort of peninsular position vis-à-vis the body and makes it seem to depend on itself alone—an effect intensified by the fact that the body is clothed up to the neck.[3]

In part, it is this self-sufficient and complete character of the face that enables a person to socially interact as though her body is unimportant. Simmel argued further that in order to achieve an aesthetic unity the spatial relations of any figure (whether it be a face or an entire body) have to be in line:

> For aesthetic effect, a form must embrace its parts and hold them together. Any stretching or spreading of extremities is ugly because it interrupts and weakens their connection with the center of the phenomenon; that is, it weakens the perceivable domination of the mind over the circumference of our being. The large gestures of baroque figures, whose limbs appear to be in danger of breaking off, are repugnant because they disavow what is properly human—the absolute encompassment of each detail by the power of the central ego.[4]

If Simmel is correct, perhaps the figure of the fat person is aesthetically unappealing because it looks dispersed, uncoordinated, beyond any central guidance. In this sense, disembodiment is closely related not only to the problem of desexualization but also to the problem of control in the fat person's life. It is as though the body has broken away from the mind. But in this collapse of integrity that many project onto the fat person, at least the face is spared. The face is often the last part of the body to be pushed out of shape by obesity. The implication of "such a pretty face" is that the face is still unspoiled, in proportion, excepted from the distortion of the rest of the body as it sits atop it self-sufficient and complete. Many people who are only moderately fat have faces that are normal in appearance. It is as though excess weight, by striking the face last, spares the most important part. Simmel points out that the face is less affected by gravity than the rest of the body and that it expresses the soul, which is itself unified and synthetic. Because of these special properties, even those faces that are rounded by fat retain a quality of integrity when this has been lost in the rest of the body. But to preserve this effect of the face, the person must dissociate it and herself from the offending body as much as possible.

The experience of being disembodied is not limited to fat people, though fat people have it most acutely. Our tendency as we age to ignore physical changes and to see ourselves as we looked when we were young is very much the same, and so is the experience of many pregnant women who regard their bodies as alien and disconnected from themselves. As the body becomes increasingly distanced from the self, the person progressively narrows the range of what she pays attention to. In order to disattend to her body, she closes off channels of information in order to avoid confronting it. This is why fat people dislike shopping for new clothes.

> Buying clothes brings you face to face with the way you fool yourself and also the reality that you are fat. You refuse to buy the clothes that fit because actually admitting that an 18 is what fits makes it all too plain. But on the other hand the 16 doesn't really fit, and there you are, lying to yourself and having the lie disproved right in front of you. *(Ellin)*

Mirrors at home are usually safer to look in than unfamiliar ones because the person can control what she sees either by eliminating full-length mirrors or by learning how to prepare for and manipulate her reflection. But the self-reflection one gets from unfamiliar mirrors is not subject to this kind of censorship. For this reason fat (and aging) people are often shocked by their images in photographs or their unanticipated reflections in plateglass windows.

Characteristically, the fat person makes a point of ignoring her body, but when it demands her attention she treats it like a foreign object. At worst, her body is so alien that she cannot even drag it along. In contemplating this, we are reminded of Simmel's point that there is something horrifying in a body that has broken away from the ego. An example is provided by a member of Overeaters Anonymous who was so obese (over 400 pounds) that she was incapable of moving without assistance:

> I couldn't get out of the reclining chair by myself. I didn't get dressed because, you see, I couldn't dress myself. My daughter was fifteen years old and going to school. School started at eight o'clock in the morning, and if I didn't get my butt out of the recliner I slept in (because God knows I couldn't sleep in a bed), if I didn't get up off my chair in the morning before she went to

school, then when she came home at two in the afternoon
I was still sitting there. In my nightgown. Or possibly in
a mu-mu because *that* I could manage. I could raise my
hands and let a mu-mu fall over my head. But I couldn't
get dressed by myself and if I wanted to go out my
daughter had to dress me.

That is low. You all know a parent's job is to raise
and dress and help a child, and here is my fifteen-year-
old raising and dressing me. *(Sylvia)*

The alienated body may not only be viewed as a serious
handicap that spoils the accomplishments of the face and head
or that defies control by the person. It may be experienced as
an enemy that is capable of destroying the self.

When I was pregnant with my second child I was scared
to death that I was gonna die or she was gonna die
because of the weight. The doctors came down on me
very hard not to gain so much weight but I went up to
250 pounds at full term. I was very embarrassed and
tense about it. The doctors would make half jokes—half-
serious comments—like "That's not just the baby in
there. That's the baby and the carriage and the infant
seat." They said, "Let's hope it's not a boy because girls
are generally smaller and you're gonna have a big baby."
Then they decided by sounding my uterus in the eighth
month that it was probably twins, and then they told me
it wasn't

I did get toxemia at the end of the pregnancy and they
put me in the hospital and induced labor. The last two
weeks I was feeling so bad—my ankles were swollen and
I couldn't put my ring on. My blood pressure was up
sixty points and I had signs of toxemia and was told to
check into the hospital. It was a very hard delivery. I was
in the transition phase of labor fully dilated for five
hours. They couldn't get her out and had to do an
emergency Caesarean when her heart beat got faint. I was
scared out of my mind. I felt either I would die or the
baby would die because I'm this awful fat person. *(Joan
Bauer)*

Although an alienated fat body is obviously a serious liability, it must also be appreciated that, for some, it serves an opposite purpose as a buffer between the self and the injurious world. In his early analysis of schizophrenia,[5] R. D. Laing talked of the "divided self," in which there was such a disrelationship between the mind and the body that the person was "unembodied," living only an inner life, or else a double life in which the body or outer appearance represents a false self as opposed to the true, hidden, inner one. In both cases the integrity of the true self is protected against the dangerous impinging outer reality by its dissociation with the physical self. No matter what happens to the physical self, it doesn't really matter because the true self is unexposed.

The relevance of Laing's analysis of schizophrenia to the situation of all young women was pointed out by Meredith Tax,[6] who described what it is like to be a woman walking down the street exposed to stares, evaluations, sexual fantasies, and comments by construction workers. Tax argued that this everyday experience is so dehumanizing that women necessarily split their bodies from their minds. If we are vulnerable to the negative judgments of our audience, we may hate our bodies and consider our minds to be our real self: then, it doesn't matter what criticisms are leveled at our bodies. Alternatively, we may manipulate and use our bodies as objects and instruments to please others. In either case, like Laing's schizophrenics we split ourselves in two as a necessary strategy for self-protection in a situation that is inhospitable.

Tax argued that Laing's analysis is relevant to all women, but clearly the process is considerably intensified with the extra vulnerability of being fat. To be rid of the body is finally one way to be rid of the impossible binds we are forced into.

A dramatic illustration of this process was related to me by a woman who had formerly been a prostitute. Because she was overweight, she had been denied sexual attention from men and pursued confirmation of her attractiveness in ways that subjected her body to abuse, injury, and degradation. Yet throughout it all, she retained a fantasy that all of these things weren't really happening to her:

Being fat made me foolhardy in some ways—I felt protected by my fat, as if no one would notice me and I would do things like walk alone in Harlem at one o'clock in the morning.

One night, walking around Harlem I got raped. The guy had a knife in my back and I was afraid I was going to get killed afterwards. So I told him he was attractive and could have sex with me without raping me. I didn't want him to be afraid of me. He took me to his house and afterwards he walked me to the subway—I guess he didn't want anyone else getting what he had. I think he even gave me a token for the subway.

If you despise your body the way I did, it doesn't matter much what happens to it as long as your self—your life—isn't injured. My body and myself were two different things and I thought all of this flesh wasn't really me—Me was something else deep inside. I didn't accept the fat as part of me until much later when I was involved in women's liberation. *(Margaret O'Connor)*

Women are prone to disembodiment not only because they are constantly exposed to intrusive judgments about their bodies but also because they are taught to regard their bodies as passive objects others should admire. Unlike men who are raised to *express themselves* unself-consciously through physical activity and sports, women's bodies are employed to be looked at. And as our culture increasingly stresses physical fitness the sense of disembodiment already present in the fat person becomes intensified.

In order to reestablish connection with their alienated bodies, to become re-embodied, women can learn to express themselves, like men, in assertive movements. Joan Bauer, who used to feel connected with her body only when she ate, discovered that she can diet more successfully if she exercises regularly, since this reduces the need for food to create the connection. As part of the re-embodiment process she also forces herself to look in the mirror and to buy clothes, making herself acknowledge the reality of her body and the fact that she consists of more than a mind.

The OA member who was unable to lift herself from her chair or get dressed unassisted felt a dramatic change as soon as she was forced by her sponsor and fellow OA members to cease treating her body as though it were invisible:

My sponsor said to me, "Sylvia, wash and set your hair so *you'll* feel better. Put on a little make-up so *you'll* feel

better. You know, I felt I wasn't worthy of setting my
hair—after all I was a big fat slob. Makeup? What big fat
slob wears makeup and draws attention to herself? No—
the black coat you put on, you go like this with the hair,
and you go. With a black coat they're not gonna see you.
It's 90 degrees outside and they're not gonna see you if
you're wearing a black coat!

Here in OA I was accepted. No one cared that I
weighed over 400 pounds. My sponsor wanted me to
comb my hair and make myself nice so that I'd feel
better. And I did—when I finally calmed down. I set my
hair and put on a little lipstick and went to the meeting
that night.

We had a "small" meeting of one hundred fifty that
night, and I'll tell you, if one person came over to tell
me how I looked, seventy-five did. To tell me, "Sylvia,
you're looking like a million dollars." Nobody had ever
said that to me in many, many years, not since I got
married and wore a size eight wedding dress. *(Sylvia)*

The heroine in *Lady Oracle*, too, felt herself to be invisible
as long as she was fat. As she loses weight, her facial and
sexual features gradually become noticeable and emerge into
sharper definition:

At home I spent hours in front of the mirror, watching as
my eyebrows, then my mouth, began to spread across my
face. I was dwindling. The sight of a fat person on the
street, which used to inspire fellow feeling, I now found
revolting. The wide expanse of flesh that had extended
like a sand dune from my chin to my ankles began to
recede, my breasts and hips rising from it like islands.
Strange men, whose gaze had previously slid over and
around me as though I wasn't there, began to look at me
from truck-cab windows and construction sites; a
speculative look, like a dog eyeing a fire hydrant.[7]

The heroine's problems do not vanish with her weight.
Although she remains thin, she finds new ways to disguise
herself. But in becoming re-embodied she has, for a time,
come out of hiding.

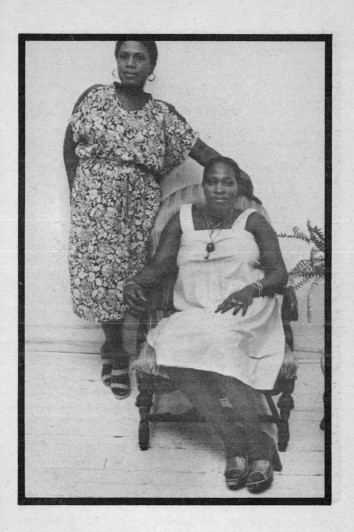

10

Before and After: Living a Postponed Life

"Kill me, oh, kill me!" said the poor creature, and bowing his head towards the water he awaited his death. But what did he see reflected in the transparent water?

He saw below him his own image, but he was no longer a clumsy dark gray bird, ugly and ungainly; he was himself a swan! . . .

He felt quite shy, and hid his head under his wing; he did not know what to think; he was so happy, but not at all proud; a good heart never becomes proud. He thought of how he had been pursued and scorned, and now he heard them all say that he was the most beautiful of all beautiful birds. The lilacs bent their boughs right down into the water before him, and the bright sun was warm and cheering, and he rustled his feathers and raised his slender neck aloft, saying with exultation in his heart, "I never dreamt of so much happiness when I was the Ugly Duckling!"

—Hans Christian Andersen

A woman may distance herself not only from her body but also from her present life. Because her unacceptable body comes to stand in her mind for everything wrong in her life, she also imagines that being fat is the cause of all her troubles. Her response is to cease living in the present. Instead, she turns all her thoughts and attentions to the future when she shall be slender. Her present self and her present life circumstances are discounted as temporary, preparatory, not the real thing. Real life, she reasons, will start after she loses weight.

The belief in a "before-and-after" transformation is a towering and universal fantasy. The ugly duckling becomes a beautiful swan. Sleeping Beauty and Cinderella are discovered and rescued by the love of a prince. The Frog Prince is redeemed by a kiss and assumes the noble appearance he was always meant to have. The hero or heroine who appeared before all the world as repulsive and unimportant is finally revealed as beautiful, lovable, and very special.

Many people believe that a particular deficiency, circumstance, or problem has kept them from realizing their potential. They are convinced that when this circumstance is overcome everything in their lives will change. The culprit can take different forms: the wrong spouse, the wrong job, the wrong house. But while this assumption applies to all kinds of people and troubles, it has special importance for fat people and their belief that only weight stands between them and their dreams. This is natural, for a fat child's social failure does come so early, so cruelly, and so specifically because of a particular physical characteristic. And starting from childhood, the belief in future transformation is encouraged by well-meaning adults who tell the fat child that she has only "baby fat," that she will "grow out of it," that inside every fat person there is a thin person waiting to come out, and that she has "such a beautiful face," and all the potential for great beauty.

Whereas other stigmatized characteristics (such as a physical deformity or an "ugly" face), do not lend themselves to fantasies of before and after, obesity does. The fat person is always theoretically capable of getting rid of her problem: weight can be lost, transformation achieved. Thus, many fat people, assuming life will start in earnest after they are thin, postpone living.

It is frequently observed in NAAFA that few fat women have a nice winter coat—they don't want to make the investment until they lose weight. Other postponements are more serious—a delay of effort to find a good job or to build a satisfying social life. Even when an overweight woman has what others are seeking, she may dismiss it as not yet counting because she hasn't yet discovered what she can do or have when she is thin:

> I've lived with three men and had lots of attention from other men, but I always think these men don't really count because my choices won't count until I'm thin.
> *(Claire Stewart)*

Promise of a great and beneficial transformation is, of course, the drawing card of all organizations devoted to weight loss. Even programs without strong religious overtones like Overeaters Anonymous appeal to the popular wish to believe that suffering can be eliminated simply by losing weight. The monthly magazine *Weight Watchers* (published by the diet organization of the same name) is essentially constructed around the fantasy of before-and-after: there are "then-and-now" photographs sent in by successful dieters, before-and-after letters to the editors, and a before-and-after feature cover story almost every month.

Sometimes they tell the story of a public figure whose life embodies the fantasy. The television actress Valerie Harper was featured in July 1975 with the suggestion that when "Rhoda" lost 25 pounds she was able to graduate from her role as dumpy sidekick on the "Mary Tyler Moore Show" to the successful and attractive star of her own weekly program.

In *Weight Watchers* magazine even the weight loss of ordinary people is accompanied by the fulfillment of their romantic dreams and a dramatic ascent up the ladder of success. In the August 1975 issue a fat secretary who loses weight realizes her dream to be a Playboy bunny. Not only does she now have a great job where she can "mix and mingle" with all kinds of interesting people, but losing weight has also made her more interesting and articulate. She is pictured "in a heavy moment of reading" and tells us that she likes to talk about philosophy and current events. And one of her secret hobbies is studying difficult vocabulary words so she'll know what they mean when people use them.

In October 1977 we read of an unhappily married fat housewife who becomes a lonely, divorced, unnoticed, dumpy woman sitting behind the secretarial desk of a theatrical agency, watching the beautiful people go by. She joins Weight Watchers, becomes slim, and now her life takes off. She is offered a fabulous new job in show business. She is dating a gorgeous Englishman with a manor house in England, and the people she meets now are "different"—more sophisitcated, more interesting, better looking. As the story closes, she is still waiting for her Prince Charming. Meanwhile, she will work to rescue other fat secretaries by convincing them to join Weight Watchers.

In real life the transformation is rarely so fully realized. More often the person loses some weight but not as much as she wants, and usually she regains part or all of it. Many who lose weight still see themselves as fat for quite a long time, and some live forever with the memory, like a prison record. But those who lose a great deal of weight do have an experience of being transformed. For one thing, the woman who goes from being fat to thin encounters great changes in the ways she is treated in the social world. Several told me that when they lost weight, people were nicer, more friendly toward them and this enabled them to act in kind. In contrast, some felt more powerful, less vulnerable when they lost weight and therefore also felt less obliged to be ingratiating, forever cheerful and anxious to please.

The experience of being reborn after a significant weight loss is generally described in euphoric terms. Yet newly thin people also frequently feel vulnerable or disillusioned. Stripped of their old bodies, they feel exposed and confused by the different set of reactions and experiences they encounter. But even worse, they are unprepared for the disappointment for all the things that *don't* change after they become thin.

The complexities of the before-and-after weight-loss experience are explored in the reflections of a young woman who literally risked her life to become slim. Susan Kanter is a twenty-nine-year-old assistant dean of admissions at a college in southern California.

Three years ago, Susan underwent intestinal bypass surgery—a procedure that disengages most of the small intestines and some of the large intestines from the digestive process (a loop is created around a large portion of the intestines). The operation is meant to minimize the amount of food absorbed so that most of what is eaten passes out of the body quickly. This allows the person to eat as much as she or he wants and still to lose weight.

It is a controversial operation. There is a significant mortality risk, and serious medical complications frequently occur, as well as prolonged discomfort from diarrhea and nausea. The operation is not generally considered to be medically justifiable unless the candidate's life is threatened by obesity and all other reducing methods have failed. It is a measure taken only by desperate people who see no other choice; this was the state of mind that Susan had reached.

She lost 105 pounds after surgery. She is short (five feet, one inch) and her weight dropped from 231 to 126, making her physically a very different person from the one she was before. In our conversation, Susan reflected on how the changes that took place in her life compared with her original expectations.

Susan Kanter

I grew up in Los Angeles, in a Jewish family with lots of eating. My father is an oral surgeon. I was a skinny kid but I started to gain small amounts of weight when I was around seventeen. I would go up and down about 20 or 25 pounds. When I had bad experiences in life I would eat to console myself.

By bad experiences I mean, for example, when I was eighteen I got pregnant and had an illegal abortion—this was before abortions were legal. I started to hemorrhage after the abortion, and the abortion wasn't completed anyway. When my mother called a doctor he said I could only get into a hospital and get medical care if my mother was willing to be criminally charged for bringing me to an abortionist. So my mother and I went to Japan forty-eight hours later, and I had the abortion there.

When we came home I had a minor nervous breakdown—I just felt pain inside. My mother freaked out and said, "You have no idea what you've done to me." And then she left me and my sister (my parents were separated) and went to Palm Springs for six months, leaving us alone. I went to a psychiatrist but he was my father's therapist and a friend of the family. So I didn't really get any help in therapy.

That was the summer of 1967, and I started hanging out with a group of hippies, and over the summer I gained 50 pounds. I was miserable about it and sensitive: for example, I would never use the word fat. I got fatter and fatter until I weighed 231 when I was 26. I was miserable when I was fat. When you're that fat you're so recognizable and noticed, and people think that fat people are mentally handicapped.

I *was* a hostile person when I was fat. I was angry and hated everybody and everything. If I had a problem at work, instead of saying, "There's a problem—what can we do about it?" I'd walk in assuming they wouldn't solve the problem. I'd be snotty and nasty—I wasn't conscious of being like that but since I hated myself, I expected a negative response and it was all I could do. The world would be hostile to me and then I'd be hostile back. And the world is really hostile to you when you're fat.

Once I walked into the lingerie department of Saks Fifth Avenue and I was just looking around. A saleslady walked up to me and said, "I'm sorry—we don't carry your size." This was completely unsolicited. I hadn't asked to try anything on. I said to the saleslady, "You know, we fat people like to look at nice things too."

When I was twenty-six I became very sick—I was paralyzed on one side, and my sickness was at first misdiagnosed as leukemia, but what really caused the paralysis was a blocked artery from taking birth-control pills.

After this sickness I had another big weight gain. I had found a nice doctor—a woman internist. She told me I had to lose weight or either I'd die or I'd have a stroke and be like a vegetable. She asked me if I had ever considered having a bypass operation and I told her no.

I had heard about the operation from my mother who had already found everything else for me to try. I tried the Stillman diet, shots, behavior therapy, pills. I went to three psychiatrists. When I was nineteen I was even hospitalized for forty-eight days of supervised starvation. I lost 51 pounds then and gained back 61.

After the doctor told me I could have a stroke and become like a vegetable I went home and cried and looked at myself in the mirror. I have always felt that I should be able to control my weight through my own effort, but I remember I said to myself that day maybe I *can't* do it by myself. So I called back the doctor and told her to find someone to do the operation. I said, if you think I should do it, I will.

She found a surgeon who seemed to have fewer complications with his patients than the others. He kept me waiting for two hours when I went for my appointment, but I liked him. I had the operation just ten days later—and spent five out of the ten days at UCLA medical library reading everything I could about it. I wanted to know everything about it, including all the problems, but I felt I had to have the operation because it was my last hope.

The night before surgery I had to have several enemas. My father came to see me in the hospital the night before the operation—he was the last one to see me—and he cried and said, "Why am I letting you do this? I'm scared for you. You can still change your mind and not have the operation." After he left I went to see a boy on another floor who had the operation a few days before, and he told me that it didn't hurt.

After the operation I did throw up every day for six weeks. It was hard for me because I hated throwing up. It was because of a lack of potassium, and once I took a potassium supplement I felt better. But there was a four-day period when I was so sick I thought I would have to have the operation reversed and have my intestines rehooked. That was three years ago.

My husband took pictures of me the day before I had surgery and we didn't pick them up until I had lost 50 pounds. I went into the store and got the pictures while he sat in the car—I wanted to see them first, alone. I was really shocked when I saw them. I had never thought I was that fat. I had known they would be horrible but I never knew I was *that* fat.

I showed them to my husband and he also said, "Susan, you were never that fat." My husband never noticed my fat—he sees only my insides. Only my mother saw the way I was fat.

I lost 105 pounds in a year. I still have no idea what I look like. Once I walked by a large window and saw the reflection in it, I was looking at it, and I didn't know it was me. When I have to walk through tight spaces like cars in a parking lot, I never know if I'll fit. In most of the dreams I have I'm fat. I weigh myself three times a day because I'm afraid my weight will go up, even though I know it can't go up. Sometimes when I look in the mirror I feel fat, and sometimes I feel thin. I become aware of how distorted my perceptions are when I pick up clothes and say "It won't fit me" and it turns out it's two sizes too big.

One day I went to see the woman who owned a store that was next door to a store I used to own—I used to be friendly with her. So I went in and looked at her and said, "Will you help me?" She said, "Yes?" I said, "I wanted to say hello." She didn't know who I was. She said I looked familiar but she didn't recognize me. I told her I didn't want to tell her who I was—I wanted to let her discover it. And I said, "If I were 105 pounds fatter, would you know who I was?" It still took her five minutes and then her mouth dropped when she realized who I was.

When I first lost weight I used to go into Saks and try on evening clothes and the saleslady would rush over to help me. I even went back to that same lingerie department in Saks and told the same saleslady I needed new underwear, and she said, "What are you, a size five?"

But it's a brief happiness. I used to think not being fat would mean instant happiness; none of that happened—it got worse.

Two years ago, a year after my operation, I was in San Francisco visiting my sister and we went to a street fair and there was a guy—an artist—who was very handsome and had beautiful paintings. My sister was half flirting with him and he was really coming on to me. It took me an hour to realize it because I have always felt, "Who would come on to you?" My mother used to say to me, "What man could look at you and love you?"

Finally he made it clear that he was interested in me. I felt adrenaline, panic, exposed, naked. Like all the people could see when they couldn't before. He was coming to L.A. and wanted to see me. I was married but I had never had this happen before. A few weeks later I got a postcard that he was coming. I decided I'd go out with him. I met him and we had a drink and I felt terrified and I realized I didn't know what to do. He thought I was neat, and I ran home. Anyone finding me attractive makes me feel vulnerable. That part still hasn't been resolved for me.

My husband, Tim, and I have been together for a long time. At this point I've arrived at a plateau and I wonder why I'm there but I just let things happen. The therapist I'm seeing is against my marriage—he thinks it's a terrible marriage but it's familiar to me. And familiar misery is better than opening yourself up to something strange and possibly hurtful. I have a terror that no one else would love me if I left my husband. I've made progress in lots of areas, but not in thinking I'm worthwhile and attractive or that men could love me.

My husband uses me. I'm a meal ticket to him. It's like living with a brother—noncommittal and pleasant. He's a student and I work to support us. When I work, the money is for both of us. If he gets a summer job when school is out, the money is just for him.

After I lost the bulk of my weight, Tim became hostile and cold to me. He was sick and tired of people paying so much attention to me and telling me how good I looked. I wasn't prepared for this—I was prepared only for good things. I thought my husband would be so happy for me—but he wasn't glad. He didn't care if I was thin or fat, but it bothers me and I really think he loved me more when I was fat—I was no threat when I was fat. I had few friends and little contact with the world.

Now I have friends and I also like to be by myself. My husband loves me less because he wants me to be dependent on him. He's dependent on me for money. When we got married I had a trust fund of fifty-four thousand dollars, and now there's only eleven hundred left. I work ten hours every day and when I go home I do the cooking and cleaning. He's a student for three or four hours a day but he's convinced he works harder than I do. All I know is that when I leave for work in the morning he's still sleeping and when I come home he's been back from school for four hours.

My relationship with my mother didn't improve either. My mother hates fat people, and I always thought if I lost weight she would love me, but I found out she's never going to love me. In therapy I found out that the person inside me who needed to be fat was a little girl who needed love and to be safe, but the fat kept people away from me.

After I lost most of my weight I got all dressed up and went to see my mother. I had lost 105 pounds, and she said to me, "Well, you could still lose a little more." I realized it was all in her mind—I couldn't do anything to make her like me.

My sister, who was also fat, went with my mother to the Orient on a vacation and she got amoebic dysentery and lost 40 pounds, she was so sick. And my mother said, "Good. I hope you lose 50."

Now my mother is fat for the first time in her life because she's been sick and bedridden. Her clothes fit me, they don't fit her. When I saw her recently she said, "Go on. Tell me how horrible I look." I just said, "I don't love you any less or more because you're fat."

People don't understand what it's like to lose weight. When the flesh leaves you, that part of you is still there—you still think you're fat and ugly and that no one can love you. My mother always said if I were thin, I'd be happy. The whole world expects you to be happy—it's hard to explain that you're not. There are some good things. It's easier for me to get around—I can walk up hills without puffing and not be looked at. But I had so much banking on thinking I would be happy. It was a fantasy. You think it's this monumental thing. I'm not fat anymore—I'm thin. Well, so is everyone else—it's not such a big deal. It's terrible to find out all the things you thought were true aren't so. I've lost most of my illusions. I don't know if life was better with the fantasy, or knowing now it was only a fantasy.

The fantasy of transformation goes to the very core of the problem of being fat and leads to a basic explanation of why weight loss is often so unsatisfying and so impermanent. Because they have always blamed all their troubles on being fat, overweight people are unprepared for the other obstacles they must face when they have overcome the most obvious one. If being fat is a symptom of a deeper problem, simply losing weight is not going to change the picture. One need not be fat to construct barriers to being loved nor to wind up feeling abused or rejected. There are many other ways of achieving the same effect. As Susan Kanter discovered, the surgical intervention meant she could change her symptoms without working out the underlying difficulties. The operation could no sooner solve some of Susan's problems than redemption by a rescuer: both are outside agents and change and self-acceptance must also come from within. The before-and-after fantasy is doomed to fail for other reasons, too.

In fairy tales the transformation is accomplished only by redemption through the unconditional love of another person. Only when the hero or heroine is recognized as truly special and worthy of special effort by someone who sees through the barriers or outer poverty do her true beauty and value come to the surface. The redeemer must be willing and able to overcome obstacles, fight his way through forests, be undaunted by ragged clothes or a repulsive appearance, if he or she is to be worthy of love and be capable of effecting the transformation. The stories are at bottom about redemption through love that endures all negative conditions.

The fat person, too, is often waiting for the person who can see their real beauty, who will love them *despite* their weight. Their excess weight serves as the test of the redeemer's worthiness. When they have been recognized and loved in their most despicable form, they are released from their curse or spell to fulfill their potential. As in the fairy tales, the test of the lover is required because of the need for unconditional love. But why does the fat person insist on love that is unconditional?

The answer is that the fat person has experienced too little love or only love that is *too* conditional. First her parents and then the world at large have told her that she is not acceptable or lovable. Now she continues to seek in adulthood the kind of unconditional acceptance that is normally extended only to children. But outside of fairy tales this kind of love is hard to find, especially for a woman seeking love from a man. Men are more likely to seek out women who will minister to *their* failings rather than women who themselves require healing.

The enormous need created by the original rejection also explains another major element of the before-and-after fantasy:

the belief in the *extraordinary* and special nature of the self. Like Cinderella or the Frog Prince, the fat person lives with a double identity. Her present self-in-the-world may be fat, ugly, despised, or disregarded, but inside, carefully nourished, is a private future self that is beautiful, powerful, lovely. The poignancy of the expression "such a pretty face" derives from the individual's involvement with her potential magnificence and the tragedy of its entrapment. Many fat women wistfully remark: "I've been told that I'm so beautiful that if I were thin I would stop traffic when I walked down the street." The need to be extraordinarily beautiful is related to the need for unconditional love. So severe was the original rejection and injury, that it is not enough to be average.

> Getting thin was always associated with all sorts of good things happening. Yes, I would get a boyfriend; yes, I would be really beautiful; yes, everyone, especially my mother, would approve of me. Each time I lost weight I gained it back. I guess when I first went to college it was all the pressure of going to a place where I was an outcast, where I was too heavy to meet boys, where everything was new. When I came back thin from Europe it was being faced with all these men in Cambridge and knowing I wasn't going to get one really. And in New York, the same thing: getting thin, wearing sexy clothes, then not meeting anyone, having awful jobs. As I've gotten thin this time, I'm much more aware of all the reasons I'm afraid of it, more aware of what being fat meant to me: how now I feel shrunk, how I feel less sexual, really, how I feel like everyone else, that I won't be special, that I won't be noticed. When I had fantasies of me thin before I was always the most beautiful, loved woman in the world. Now I have to look in the mirror and not see anything so remarkable. *(Ellin)*

As Ellin realized, her need to be special was so strong that given the choice between admitting she was ordinary, or tolerating great pain in being fat to preserve the fantasy of potential greatness, she chose the latter. Again, *Lady Oracle* provides a neat illustration of how a sense of greatness may be linked in fantasy with the pains of being fat.

The heroine, Joan, recalls that her mother brought her to

ballet class in the hopes that she would slim down. At the age of seven she was to take part with other children in the ballet school's annual spring recital, which included her favorite number, "The Butterfly Frolic." This dance involved wearing her beloved costume, a gauzy ballerina skirt and butterfly wings. Joan's mother, however, was disturbed by the appearance of her fat daughter in so skimpy an outfit. Just before the performance she convinces the dance teacher to remove her from the *corps de ballet* so as not to spoil the effect that the other children produce. The teacher then gives Joan a "special" part: since she's the brightest, instead of being a butterfly like the other girls she will instead be a "mothball." Instead of wearing a gauzy butterfly and wings she will wear a white teddy-bear costume and a large sign around her neck saying "mothball."

Our heroine weeps and begs to be left in the *corps,* but she is given only this choice: she can be the mothball or nothing at all. Finally, she is pushed onto the stage to dance her piece:

At the right moment Miss Flegg gave me a shove and I lurched onto the stage, trying to look, as she had instructed me, as much like a mothball as possible. Then I danced. There were no steps to my dance, as I hadn't been taught any, so I made it up as I went along. I swung my arms, I bumped into the butterflies, I spun in circles and stamped my feet as hard as I could on the boards of the flimsy stage, until it shook. I threw myself into the part, it was a dance of rage and destruction, tears rolled down my cheeks behind the fur, the butterflies would die; my feet hurt for days afterwards. "This isn't me," I kept saying to myself, "they're making me do it"; yet even though I was concealed in the teddy-bear suit, which flopped about me and made me sweat, I felt naked and exposed, as if this ridiculous dance was the truth about me and everyone could see it. The butterflies scampered away on cue and much to my surprise I was left in the center of the stage, facing an audience that was not only laughing but applauding vigorously. Even when the beauties, the tiny thin ones, trooped back for their curtsey, the laughter and clapping went on, and several people, who must have been fathers rather than mothers, shouted, "Bravo, mothball!"[1]

In this story, the source of Joan's misery is also the feature that brings her special recognition and applause; the two are inextricably tied. Many of us, like fairy-tale characters, try to convince ourselves that our current tribulations will turn out to have been a blessing, for they will prepare us to receive more gracefully the glory that awaits us.

Originally, we develop a belief in our potential greatness in order to console ourselves for not being loved or accepted, but eventually the preservation of the fantasy seems to take precedence over being loved in fact. It is not just our selves that we dignify and glorify in our fantasies, but life itself. In our dreams of before and after, life seems more intense, more exciting, more just than it is in reality. In our fantasies we make more of life than it could ever offer us in fact. Eventually, reality often seems unworthy of the effort.

In the long run, we must change the oppressive attitudes and structures of our society that force so many of us (and not just the overweight) into a life of daydreams and isolation. If any point is made by the stories told here, it is that human potential and happiness are tragically wasted by our society's emphasis on physical beauty. When the fat person is set apart from the world, defined as deviant and defiant, this division and conflict are internalized and reproduced within her. Social stigma almost inevitably produces self-hatred. Slave mentality can be eliminated only by ending slavery.

At the same time, we must also struggle to change the personal adaptations we have made to an oppressive situation. The needs to be extraordinary, special, unconditionally accepted must be relinquished, for they keep us from enjoying the accomplishments and pleasures the real and present life does have to offer.

There is no denying that being fat in our society means living with a substantial handicap. But even more important than losing weight is giving up the fantasies associated with it, whether we weigh 120 or 220 or 420. In this, both NAAFA and Overeaters Anonymous are correct. For one thing, unless we do, even being slender is unlikely to bring happiness or to be sustained. For another, although our fantasies are initially comforting, they progressively destroy our lives. How?

First, the fantasy of before and after is predicated on an assumption of passivity and inaction, consistent with other features of women's oppression. At first glance, this would not seem to be the case. After all, part of the appeal of before-and-after photographs is their celebration of the will—the power we have to recreate ourselves in our own desired image. But the before-and-after fantasy has a different impact on men and women.

Because physical appearance is so consequential for women, we attempt to change our looks in order to change our lives, while in our places men would think about their work or achievements in the world. Although both pursuits can become ungratifying and alienating, the focus on physical appearance is more trivial, more unrealistic, more certain to maintain us as objects rather than subjects. Like Sleeping Beauty or Cinderella, we wait for a worthy man to tell us we are beautiful, for beauty is a title that is conferred by others, not earned by ourselves.

Second, the before-and-after fantasy encourages us to wait and postpone living until we have indeed wasted our potential. It is the last thing we need. Women are always put in the position of having to wait: first we wait for the right man to come along, and then we wait for him to pay attention to us when he is finished with work. After that, we wait on our children.

The Sleeping Beauty is rewarded for her infinite patience: she waits a hundred years, but she gets a prince, and she doesn't grow even a day older in all this time. In fairy tales time may not run out when animation is suspended; in our fantasies time may stop when we put ourselves on the shelf until we are slender or chosen. But in reality, life slips by.

In the end, the activity of postponing life is profoundly debilitating. This is obvious in the stories we have heard. At first, the faith in transformation brings excitement, anticipation, great expectations. But when losing weight and starting to live are postponed until tomorrow and tomorrow, hopefulness turns into resignation and immobility. It is characteristic. First there are only twenty pounds to lose and they are lost easily and often. But the gap between what we are and what we must become before we can start to live progressively widens as obesity increases, as it almost always does. Soon it is fifty pounds and later more that must be lost. Transformation seems increasingly remote, but rather than give up the fantasy, we actually slow down and bring to a halt our life's effort itself.

It is hard to give up the fantasy that we are extraordinary, that we can find unconditional love, that life is ultimately just and will reward us for undeserved suffering and uncomplaining patience. It is hard to get into the running after watching from the sidelines as a spectator or confidante. But only by entering the present world, in whatever flawed condition, can we live at all.

Appendix I:
Methods

Some readers may wonder how I did the research for this book, and what my relationship was to the people and the organizations I've written about.

The autobiographical accounts and quotations are taken from long open-ended interviews I conducted with people who identified themselves as having a problem with or concern about weight. I interviewed about fifty people in depth (for four hours or longer) and had shorter conversations with many others.

I found and selected these people in a variety of ways. Over a period of two years while I did the research for the book I discussed it with colleagues and friends and presented preliminary ideas to a number of audiences (women's groups, professional conferences, research seminars). In response, several people spontaneously told me how relevant the subject was to their lives and volunteered to be interviewed themselves. Others told me of friends, relatives, or acquaintances who would be interesting to talk with. In these cases, I usually asked my informants to ask the potential interviewee whether she or he would be willing to talk, and if the response was affirmative (it almost always was) I pursued the opportunity. Several people I interviewed later called me with the names of other people they knew who had expressed interest in the project. In a few instances I was referred to subjects by people working in the area of weight control (for example, several of the men I describe in Appendix II were referred to me by a physician and a nutritionist).

Since I used an informal network-of-acquaintances approach in finding and interviewing people for the study, I cannot claim with any statistical certainty that they are representative of the American population. But the themes I have explored appeared with such frequency and consistency in these conversations that I myself have no doubt of it.

I explained to each that I was writing a book about the experience of being overweight, and that I wanted to learn about the significance that weight had held in his or her life. Except in three or four cases I used a tape recorder. The exceptions sprang from the fact that I talked with some people while traveling without a tape recorder. I could therefore study these conversations and think about what was most important in them. In two cases ("Ellin" and a portion of "Rose Daniels") the excerpts are drawn from already-written unpublished autobiographies, which the writers generously offered to me.

The autobiographical accounts I have included are considerably shorter than the original interviews, but in selecting what to include from these conversations I tried to be faithful to the spirit of each story as well as to focus on material that best illustrated the issues and patterns I was describing and analyzing. Similarly, in selecting illustrative cases from a much larger set of interviews, I tried to represent all the experiences that seemed important while focusing on the most articulate or interesting speakers. All excerpts are direct quotations from the interviews. I changed nothing but names and a few biographical details (such as place of residence or occupation) where this was necessary to protect someone's privacy.

I chose to observe and write about the National Association To Aid Fat Americans, Overeaters Anonymous, and the summer diet camp for overweight children not only because they are rich sources of information about the experience of being overweight but also because they illuminate different sides of the subject. By looking at both OA and NAAFA, one is forced to confront both the psychological and political dimensions of the experience of being overweight. The study of the diet camp, on the other hand, allows us to see how people are socialized into the identity of being a fat person.

Sensing that these were fruitful social worlds to study, I explained my research interests to the owner of Camp Laurel (a pseudonym) and the president and some of the executive officers of NAAFA. In both cases I was given permission to observe these settings and helpful introductions to their participants. I explained to all the people I talked with at the camp and at NAAFA that I was a sociologist writing a book about what it is like to be fat and about some of the organizations that overweight people join.

Because of the special nature of Overeaters Anonymous (relying on small group meetings of anonymous participants) I felt I couldn't observe it as directly as I could study NAAFA or Camp Laurel, for I thought that the presence of a sociologist-observer might disrupt the process of these groups. I do not believe in covert or disguised research and thus did not feel that I could join the organization as just another member in order to observe the meetings unobtrusively.

I therefore attempted to find out about OA by attending a few meetings conducted specifically for people who are considering joining the organization. At one of these meetings I purchased some OA pamphlets and booklets describing the program, and learned that there was to be a regional (Northeast) convention of OA members at the Concord Hotel in upstate New York. Several thousand OA members would be spending the weekend attending workshops, thematic rap sessions, and marathon meetings. These sessions were conducted along the same lines as regular chapter meetings, observing the same rules and rituals. The only difference was that in participating in these discussions, OA members addressed a roomful of fellow members who were strangers rather than group members known to them.

Since the convention was open to all interested people I did not feel the same hesitation about attending these sessions as I did about observing regular chapter meetings. Undoubtedly there are some differences between local chapter meetings and what happens in conference discussions. But in the sense that OA is an organization of people who have pledged their anonymity even in local meetings and who closely follow a prescribed set of practices on every occasion, the convention discussion groups were probably not very different from ordinary chapter meetings. Certainly by attending the convention I was able to learn a great deal about OA and its significance for members.

I also learned that these meetings (and some held in previous

years) had been tape-recorded by a convention recording service and that these tapes were for sale to the public. The
sessions had been recorded with the written permission of individual speakers, so that participants who did not sign releases
were not included in the recordings. The tapes were very useful
to me in writing this book. I purchased and studied several
dozen of them, and, like the regional convention, they gave
me an opportunity to observe the organization closely and to
quote its participants without having to intrude.

Finally, since I was interested in popular conceptions of
obesity I also followed stories and news items about weight
problems that appeared in newspapers and magazines during
the years (1976–78) that I worked on the book. In this respect,
as in others, I was helped by several friends and colleagues
all over the country who clipped and mailed to me stories from
local newspapers.

Appendix II:
About
the Photographs

As a photographer, I have been interested in women and their attitudes towards their bodies. I had never before photographed very fat women, and to begin this project I had to consider different ways of finding subjects. Asking to photograph strangers for a book about being overweight could be intruding into private and painful territory. Would people think that I (not fat) would mock or sensationalize their weight? My aim was the opposite, to photograph large women who projected their beauty, grace, and sexiness. I needed the right context to explain my perspective and gain the person's trust, so I looked for situations in which people had identified themselves as fat. I attended NAAFA meetings, dances, and fashion shows over three years and got to know some of the members well. At the last annual convention I was the official NAAFA photographer. Over the course of a summer I spent time with campers and counselors at a diet camp. Most were eager to pose for pictures that would document their transformation. The before-and-after photographs of the boys were taken seven weeks apart. Some of the portraits are of women from a large-size model agency. Others are of people who answered my ad: "Woman photographer wants models size 14+ for a book about being overweight." I would like to thank Linda Ferrer, Beth Kramer, Dan McCormack, Thom O'Connor, and Ethel Virga for their contributions to this project.

Naomi Bushman

June 1979

Appendix III:
Fat Men:
A Different Story

The research reported in this book focused almost exclusively on women because it was immediately obvious to me that being fat or worrying about weight is a more consequential and meaning-laden issue for women than for men. I did, however, talk with several men as well. Their thoughts and experiences, when compared with those of the women, provide a contrast that nicely illuminates the issues we've explored throughout the book. Their stories, taken as a group, are so different from those of the women that they stand as further evidence of the close association that is drawn in our minds and in our culture between weight and sexuality and sex roles.

John Kalso, a dealer in unusual gemstones, is in business for himself in a small midwestern city. He is in his late thirties but looks a little older. Almost six feet tall and weighing close to 300 pounds, Kalso has a bear-like appearance. His wife is a slim and stylish-looking teacher. The Kalsos live in a small apartment: there is only a bedroom and a living room with a small Pullman kitchen.

The heavy drapes in the living room are always drawn shut, even in the daytime, to keep out sunlight and dust. The livingroom furniture consists of a dilapidated couch, an armchair, and a couple of folding chairs, all arranged to face the important objects of the apartment—gemstones, housed in several illuminated glass cases, some for sale and some that are Kalso's personal pieces. Kalso frequently remarks that all he wants out of his life is to enjoy his collection of gemstones in peace.

Each display case has its own corner of the room and sits under a spotlight. Here Kalso spends almost all of his time and conducts his business. He has few friends and keeps his telephone number unlisted. He is careful to protect his privacy. The only visitors to the apartment are the gemstone dealers he does business with. He spends quiet evenings lying on his couch, happily admiring his collection. He leaves the apartment a few days each week to travel around the region to auctions and estate sales where he acquires new gems to sell.

Despite what one might expect from his deep appreciation for things of beauty, Kalso is not a mild-mannered man. Indeed, he unapologetically describes himself as combative. Not a stranger to confrontation and challenge, he tolerates no hostile remarks about his weight: "People who know me know that whatever they dish out to me, they'll get back. If someone who's smaller than I am says, 'You're a fat slob,' I would say 'You know, there's nothing to stop me from breaking your jaw.' People who are stupid enough to make remarks like that should suffer the consequences. If someone insinuates something by telling me, 'I lost a hundred pounds and I feel great,' I say 'I feel great, too. And you were an asshole before you lost the weight and you're one now.'"

Kalso's style of self-defense was learned early in life, he claims, by growing up in the streets: "The big thing growing up was being able to rank out someone else. So when I was a kid, if a guy passed a remark about weight to me, I might say 'Your wife didn't mind!'"

Tom Antonova runs his own plumbing supply business in Watertown, an industrial town on the outskirts of Boston. When he was last weighed a few weeks ago, he had reached his highest weight of 525 pounds. For the past twenty days he has been on a protein-sparing fast diet (drinking only liquid protein). He estimates that he has already lost about 60 pounds, about three pounds a day. He wants to fast until he is down to 340 pounds so he can tolerate surgery, and then he wants to undergo an intestinal bypass operation.

Although he wants to undergo surgery for "health" reasons, Tom claims that he is not sensitive about his weight: "When a stranger on the street comes up to me and says, 'Hey, how much do you weigh?' I tell him. Some of my friends who are overweight have a hangup about their weight, but it doesn't bother me if someone asks. I'm not ashamed to tell them."

Wayne Johnson grew up in New York in a middle-class black family and was on the football team in high school. He now works as an administrator in a black community-action organization. Wayne has weighed as much as 411 pounds and now weighs about 330. He is six feet tall and would like to weigh 245. He explains that he doesn't think of himself as fat, but sees himself pretty much as he was as a young athlete. "When I walk down the street I see myself as a thin person. I'm always surprised when people make remarks about my size, because I don't think of myself as fat. I'd rather be fat than thin. I like being big. In my head, being big means being powerful."

Joe Golden, now sixty years old, is the owner of a fairly successful middle-sized grocery store in Oakland, California. When he was in college he played on the football team. Afterwards, when his muscle turned to flab, he gained weight, reaching a high of 283: "I was a pilot in the air force after college. I lost 50 pounds to get in, and then I gained it right back. Sometimes the guys would razz me about my weight. They'd say 'Boy, Golden, one day you'll have to bail out and the parachute won't hold you.' It didn't bother me. I'd joke back and say, 'If we bail out over the ocean I'll be in good shape.'"

The responses of these men address different aspects of being fat, but they all illustrate a striking difference between the experiences of overweight men and women. Being overweight is a more powerful and pervasive experience for a woman than for a man. In our culture, being fat more deeply affects a woman's self-image, her social identity, and her treatment by others. Even when a woman is only 20 or 30 pounds overweight, her life is often greatly affected by her weight, while men are allowed a much greater margin of weight variance before they are defined by others as "overweight" or see themselves that way. Even men who are 200 pounds overweight by conventional standards told me that being fat wasn't very important in their lives; they seemed not to think about it very much and claimed it didn't cause them suffering in work or in their personal relationships. They were obviously less self-conscious than fat women, and most important of all, many were not inclined to "psychologize" about their weight or see it as indicative of any emotional or personal problems. If being fat was considered a problem at all by men, it was mainly in terms of their concerns about health: they feared it might shorten their life span. But being fat did not spread into other parts of men's lives. Several women I interviewed pointed out that no fat women in the media or popular culture were treated with respect and admiration the way an occasional fat man was so treated. A few mentioned the famous fictional detective Nero Wolfe, who never let his work interfere with the ceremony of his meals yet who was highly respected, sought after, and catered to.

Having made the argument for differences between male and female experiences with obesity, some qualifications must be added. Many of the men I talked with had been athletes when young. Fat had been a middle-aged phenomenon. Fat childhoods did not figure in their biographies (and therefore their self-images) as it did for many of the women. Furthermore, while most of the men I interviewed were over forty, the women were somewhat younger (mainly in their thirties). The reason for this age difference is itself significant. On the whole, men did not identify themselves as having a weight problem, did not seek psychotherapy or medical help or join a diet organization (and therefore were not referred to me and my study) until they were old enough to worry about weight as a health concern. In contrast, the women identified themselves as having a problem even when (because of youth or the slight degree of obesity) health was not an issue. I do suspect that if I had talked with much younger men, the contrast between the experiences of women and men would not have been so striking. Nowadays men are starting earlier to worry about their weight and physical appearance.

Nevertheless, even now, almost all of the patients who go to diet doctors or join self-help groups to lose weight are women. Clearly, being fat is still more troublesome to and for women than it is for men. And even more important, women who are not objectively overweight are frequently preoccupied with weight in a way that normal-sized men seldom are. In a recent study of one hundred sixty middle-aged women, a sociologist found that over fifty percent responded to the question "What would you like to change about yourself?" by saying they wanted to lose weight. In most cases the women had no discernible weight problem.[1] Thus, although the men described in this chapter are not really comparable in certain respects (generation, age when they got fat) to the women, they nevertheless illuminate important differences in the experiences of fat men and women.

One contrast that is immediately apparent is the relative lack of self-consciousness of fat men and the lack of importance accorded by men to their weight as a condition of their lives. Although they were significantly overweight, several men mentioned that they were always surprised when other people or external circumstances called attention to their obesity. They didn't think of themselves as fat, and therefore were surprised when others did.

For example, James Arvin, a fifty-seven-year-old financially successful real-estate agent, explained that in retrospect he realized he had been significantly overweight (he weighed as much as 240 pounds) for over twenty years but that throughout this time he still thought of himself as basically a thin person who was temporarily overweight. What got him started on a diet was the shock he experienced when he saw himself in a home movie and he looked so much bigger than he had believed.

The comparative lack of self-consciousness expressed by men went beyond seeing themselves as basically thin people. Most of the men denied worrying about what others would think of their weight. None of the men described eating in public or shopping as shameful or embarrassing experiences as so many women did. Indeed, John Kalso, the gem dealer described earlier, often goes into a Howard Johnson's restaurant to compete with a friend in eating desserts. "We would sit there for two hours eating every dessert on the menu. I didn't care what people in the restaurant thought of me."

Several men mentioned that shopping for clothes is sometimes a nuisance because there isn't a wide selection in large sizes and the sizing is often inconsistent. But none of them described shopping as an embarrassing situation. Unlike the women, none admitted to worrying about what the sales clerks think of them. Joe Golden, for example, compared his feelings about shopping with those of his wife, who was considerably less overweight: "I think women suffer more from being overweight. If a saleslady says to my wife, 'You can't get into a size sixteen,' she feels insulted. If I go into a store and I say, 'Have you got a forty-four?' and they say no, I say, 'Don't you see, you have too many thirty-twos and not enough forty-fours.' I reprimand *them* for not having big enough sizes."

In contrast to most of the women, the men as a group could not think of many ways their weight had caused difficulty. They claimed it had not seriously affected their sexual and friendship opportunities or their sense of masculinity, nor did they think it had hurt their careers. It is clear that their perception of obesity not hurting their work opportunities is out of keeping with the facts. The smaller chance of being hired or promoted if one is overweight has been clearly documented. Perhaps it is no accident that most of these men ran their own small businesses—had they worked for companies they almost certainly could not have been so unaware of job discrimination:

John Kalso (gem dealer): In business, the only thing that matters is money. What you look like doesn't really count. As a matter of fact, my size is an asset to me when I'm buying because it intimidates people.

Tom Antonova (plumbing supplies): If anything, my weight has helped me in business. People remember me; it breaks the ice—they feel they know me because I stand out.

All of the men described in this chapter were married (with the exception of Wayne Johnson, who had been living with the same woman for several years). This is what they had to say about sexual opportunities or about whether their weight bothered their partners:

John Kalso: Before I was married, when I was dating I might have occasionally thought that a particular woman wouldn't make it with me because I was fat, but it was never said. I hope I've never cultivated relationships with women who would make a judgment about me on that basis. Certainly, I never was afraid to approach a woman because I was worried about what she thought about my weight—I've been on my own and on the streets since I was 16, so I'm not gonna worry about what someone might say. There are people, whether they are black or yellow or whatever, who use this or that for an excuse about why they don't have a job or anything else. I don't believe in that. Whether or not I ever got rejected by a

woman because I'm fat, I don't know. But when I got
rejected, I never assumed it was because of my weight,
and it didn't stop me from asking. If you want to have
something or do something there comes a time when you
have to shit or get off the pot.
I don't think my weight bothers my wife—in fact, it
probably makes her more secure. Maybe she'd worry if I
lost weight that I'd be more likely to have other women
around.

Wayne Johnson: There were probably some women who
excluded me because of my weight but I've always been
relatively successful with women and my weight didn't
inhibit me.

James Arvin: I never worried that my wife wouldn't love me
or anything because of my weight. She was concerned
about my health, not my appearance.

It is difficult not to be skeptical about the claims made by
the men that their weight caused them no grief. Some of this
might be explained as a kind of male bravado displayed to a
female interviewer. Surely the reclusiveness of John Kalso was
not so different from that described by many women I interviewed, and his public gorging on desserts and combativeness
are not unlike the social rebelliousness suggested in the accounts of the women. The difference, and it is significant, is
that John Kalso and the other men fought back, or at least
claimed to do so, while the women were characteristically self-
blaming and uncomfortable with the rebellious aspect of their
behavior.
There was one area in which several men did confess to
feeling self-conscious. It had to do with public situations where
they would appear ridiculous or vulnerable because of their
size:

Wayne Johnson: The only time I'm embarrassed about my
weight is when I'm clumsy—for example, sitting in a
chair and having it fall apart, which has happened to me.
Also, there are some chairs I just won't sit in—like a
narrow chair. I'm not going to sit in a narrow chair and

have my ass hanging over either side.
Also, when I was heavier and had a truck, the driver's
wheel would sometimes leave a mark on my shirt, and it
embarrassed me for that line to show.

John Kalso: The only thing that bothers me is booths in a
restaurant. They're all made for the 135-pound guy. I
don't want to sit with my stomach hanging over the
table. I'm on the road a lot and eat in restaurants a lot. If
restaurants only have booths I walk out. After all, I'm
paying for it. I might as well be comfortable.

One of the most interesting ways that fat men and women
differed about the place of weight in their lives was that the
men were much less introspective about it. The women tended
toward much speculation on the psychological origins or functions of their overweight, or saw weight as a symptom of an
emotional or personal problem. Most of the men overtly expressed a matter-of-fact attitude about their weight. Unlike the
men, many of the women had spent a good deal of time in
psychotherapy talking about the meaning of their weight. Some
of this difference is surely due to the relative youth of the
women. They have matured in a more introspective and psychologically oriented generation.
When the men talked about how or why they were overweight they did not suggest a psychological reason. They characteristically accounted for their situation as common to ex-
athletes who tend to gain weight when their active period is
over. Several (including Johnson and Antonova) mentioned
their ethnic backgrounds as a key factor in their eating habits,
but they did not link these ethnic traditions to underlying psychological dispositions, as the Jewish women I spoke with
typically did:

Tom Antonova: My parents were from Yugoslavia and we
ate a lot; everyone in our community did. We ate lots of
starches, breads, and potatoes. At a dinner we would
typically have spaghetti *and* bread *and* meat *and*
potatoes. My mom weighed 260 pounds when she
married my dad. My sister weighs 210. My first wife's
parents were also big. Her mother weighed 250 and her

father 300 and her brother 280. When I ate with them I'd always drink a whole quart of Pepsi—just at dinner alone.

Whatever the actual reasons for the accumulation of fat, women do tend to psychologize about it. This is important, for it means that women are also more likely to feel responsible and guilty and to see fat as a symptom of a more general failure and personality problem.

It is hard to know who is more oppressed—women who make something very significant out of their weight or men who deny their feelings—but it does at least seem true that women are terribly preoccupied with weight and much of their time and emotional energy is used up worrying about it. As in other areas of life, the men take a more instrumental approach:

John Kalso: I regard life as a vale of tears—I want to get through life like everyone else with as little aggravation as possible. One thing I don't do is place myself in antagonistic situations. I'm not going to surround myself with people who view me negatively because I'm overweight. Most people fall outside the norm on something, anyway.

In general, then, for men fat did not equal character. They did not worry that being fat really meant they didn't want sex or intimacy, or that they weren't masculine. Of course, it is generally acknowledged that men are less introspective and aware of their feelings than are women. It could thus be argued that men do indeed suffer from being fat in ways they are not conscious of. The one "character" worry occasionally expressed by men had to do with lack of will power.

For example, James Arvin described how he had frequently made bets with his tennis instructor that he would lose a certain amount of weight in an agreed-upon time period. Those bets had usually worked, because he knew he was highly motivated to meet a challenge once demonstration of his will power was at stake. He also talked of his reluctance to return to his doctor for a checkup on a prediabetic condition because he was embarrassed that he had lacked the will power to lose weight after his doctor told him he should. He never considered going to a self-help group for dieters and for a long time refused to see a doctor for help in losing weight because he thought a person should be able to do it on his own. This embarrassment at deficient will power must not be taken lightly. Although Arvin did not elaborate on why it was important to him, the shame was probably considerable given the high value placed on self-control and independence by men of his generation.

In general, men were more concerned with obesity hurting their physical health and their capacity to work than with their physical appearance. And when they did worry about what they looked like, it didn't have to do so much with women's responses as it did with the opinions of other men. They feared being fat might be associated with looking older and, in any case, make them look less powerful and authoritative in the eyes of other men:

Joe Golden: When I was in college, playing football, I
    weighed 245 pounds, but I had a thirty-eight-inch waist.
    Now, weighing the same amount, I have a forty-four-inch
    waist. The other day I was taking a walk, and there were
    three young guys hitchhiking who stopped me and asked
    me for a quarter. I said, "why don't you get a job?" and
    they called me a big fat bastard. You see, if you're fat,
    that's the first thing people go after—it's your
    vulnerability. But this never happened to me before I was
    fifty, even though I was fat before. No one called me a
    big fat bastard until I hit fifty, because now I look like I
    can't fight them anymore. If I got into a fight now I
    could have a heart attack. It's only when you get older
    and vulnerable that people use your weight as your
    Achilles' heel. Sometimes I see an acquaintance of mine,
    a man who used to be a great baseball player, and we
    always say when we were young people were respectful,
    but now they crowd us.
    I went to a young doctor and he was very insulting to
    me. He said, "You should be exercising—I run five miles
    a day." So here was this young guy showing off his
    figure to me, and I felt he was baiting me. So I said,
    "When I was your age I could *pick you up* and run five
    miles."

James Arvin: Since I've lost weight I feel much younger
    because I'm more active now, and it's when you were
    younger that you were more active.

What, then, can we make of these differences between men
and women as they talk about the place weight has in their
lives? It is not surprising that the different experiences of weight
are so closely tied up with the respective sex roles, for weight
affects the body and the different meanings bodies traditionally
have for men and women. Since women are primarily valued
as sex objects for men, their value declines when their looks
depart from media standards of desirability. Since men are
primarily evaluated as wage-earners, extra weight diminishes
their value because it is associated with aging and sickness.

In talking about their vulnerability when aging was connected with growing fat, the men were talking, I believe, about
how their weight detracted from their masculinity—even
though they were less explicit than women were in this admission. And, whereas women felt that being fat made them
less successful as women in the eyes of *men,* who were the
judges, men seemed to be saying that their excess weight diminished them as men *in the eyes of other men* rather than
women. For both men and women it is men who set the standards of sexual success and failure and men who constitute the
critical audience.

As we are all increasingly socialized to be consumers rather
than producers, men as well as women will be evaluated increasingly in terms of how they measure up to media images
of attractiveness rather than their achievements in work. Thus
men's experiences with weight will increasingly resemble those
of women. An example can be found in recent news reports.

When Elvis Presley died reporters and commentators on
popular culture repeatedly treated his weight gain in the last
years as a metaphor for his decline. The image of the famous
pelvis softened into flab was a symbol of the degeneration of
a once-towering sexual hero. This theme was drawn vividly.
Frequent mention was made, for example, of how, shortly
before his death, Elvis had humiliated himself by splitting his
too-tight pants during a performance, and all the newspaper
articles and posthumous biographies dwelt on the junk foods
he reportedly ate in huge quantities.

As I argued earlier, it seems likely that slimness is becoming more salient to men as they are increasingly evaluated according to media images of physical attractiveness. Evidence for this trend is readily apparent among gay men and in gay culture. For if any group of people worry about their weight more than American women it is probably gay men—at least those who are single and on the sexual market.

In some ways, contemporary gay culture involves an adoption, exaggeration, and even a celebration by men of women's traditional sex roles—the cultivation of domestic work such as gourmet cooking and home decoration, and especially the serious cultivation of looking fashionable, youthful, and attractive. Nowhere is this clearer than in the emphasis placed on a slim body in gay standards of male beauty. Indeed, the ideal body weight for a gay man seems to be 20 pounds below the ideal weight for a man according to heterosexual standards.

One gay man I interviewed would probably be considered average or perhaps ten pounds overweight in straight society; he pointed out that he was definitely considered overweight in the gay community. On one occasion, a man he met in a bar told him he was no longer interested in sex when he saw him undressed. He also described how in gay bars he was frequently squeezed or pinched around the waist by men who, under the guise of giving him a friendly welcome, were actually trying to determine if he was too fat. Another middle-aged man I spoke with lost 50 pounds when he separated from his wife of twenty years and came out as gay. He explained that losing a lot of weight was common among homosexual men when they first came out and added that when a homosexual man is fat, he is often viewed in the gay community as not having sufficient "self-pride." He is also suspected of not having acquired a truly political gay consciousness. Thus, overweight gay men share with all overweight women the burden of imputed psychological interpretations.

Among gay men there is a small subgroup known as "chubby chasers": men who are attracted specifically to fat men; these men are considered by the general gay community to be as strange and perverse as are men attracted to fat women in American heterosexual society.

It is hard to know whether the weight consciousness and "looksism" of gay men will soon extend to heterosexual men. Frequently gay men have anticipated styles, values, and practices that are later adapted by heterosexual men as gender roles become less sharply differentiated and men's experiences come closer to women's. Such a concern was nicely stated by Mr. Golden, the grocery-store owner described earlier in this chapter, as he worried about the future of his overweight son. His comments also remind us that for men as well as for women, being fat is increasingly associated with being from a lower social class and failing to achieve upward mobility:

My son is twenty-three years old and is being trained for hotel and restaurant management. When he left for college he was in good shape, but now he is quite heavy. I tell him it's not what's up here in the head that counts today, but what you look like. I tell him unless he loses weight he'll be a second-rate citizen. Girls who are the news announcers on television don't have a brain in their heads, but they're beautiful and they get to read the news that the smart but ugly people in the background have to write.

My son was telling me about how all the other guys were getting good jobs running hotels but they won't put my son up at the front desk. They'll put him in the back—in the kitchen. He'll probably wind up as a chef. Our society is geared to how you look. We've learned from television that the thin guy is better than the fat guy. The beautiful people will be up in the front taking all the bows and credit and the workers will be shoved in the back. My son will be shoved in the back.

Notes

Preface

1. A similar argument about mythologizing cancer has been made by Susan Sontag in her book *Illness as Metaphor* (New York: Vintage, 1978).
2. The concept of stigma has been most thoroughly explored by Erving Goffman in his book *Stigma: Notes on the Management of Spoiled Identity* (Englewood Cliffs, N.J.: Prentice-Hall, 1964).

Chapter 4

1. Margaret Atwood, *Lady Oracle* (New York: Simon and Schuster, 1976), pp. 69–71.
2. Natalie Allon, "Deviance Avowal in Daily Interactions Between Overweights and Thin Normals," unpublished paper presented to the Society for the Study of Social Problems (August 1976).
3. Atwood, *Lady Oracle*, pp. 93–94.

Chapter 5

1. A. J. Stunkard, "Obesity and The Social Environment," in *Recent Advances in Obesity Research: I,* edited by Alan Howard (Westport, Conn.: Technomic Publishing Co., 1975).
2. Anne Scott Beller, *Fat and Thin: A Natural History of Obesity* (New York: Farrar, Straus & Giroux, 1977), p. 264.
3. In a review of the medical literature on the influence of obesity on health, George Mann points out that the contribution of obesity to heart disease is small. George Mann, "The Influence of Obesity on Health," (two parts) in *The New England Journal of Medicine,* vol. 291, no. 4 (July 25, 1974) and vol. 291, no. 5 (August 1, 1974).

4. Jean Mayer, *Overweight: Causes, Cost and Control* (Englewood Cliffs, N. J.: Prentice-Hall, 1968), p. 91.
5. Beller, *Fat and Thin: A Natural History of Obesity*, pp. 37–40.
6. *San Francisco Chronicle*, December 2, 1978, p. 2.
7. Gudrun Fonfa, "Looksism as Social Control," *Lesbian Tide* (January 1975): 20.
8. Lyn Mabel-Lois, "Fat Dykes Don't Make It," *Lesbian Tide* (October 1974): 11.

Chapter 6

1. Anne Hollander, "When Fat Was in Fashion," *The New York Times Magazine*, October 23, 1977, p. 36.
2. Cesar Rotondi, *Grand Obese* (New York: St. Martin's Press, 1979), p. 48.
3. Robert Jones, "Walking into the Fire: Sarah Caldwell Comes to the Met," *Opera News*, vol. 40, no. 14 (February 14, 1976): 11–12.

Chapter 7

1. Susie Orbach makes this point in *Fat Is a Feminist Issue* (London: Paddington Press, 1978), p. 58.
2. Margaret Atwood, *Lady Oracle* (New York: Simon and Schuster, 1976), pp. 87–88.
3. Atwood, *Lady Oracle*, p. 74.

Chapter 9

1. Margaret Atwood, *Lady Oracle* (New York: Simon and Schuster, 1976), p. 121.
2. This problem was presented as a letter to the editor of *Weight Watchers* magazine, December 1974, p. 6.
3. Georg Simmel, "The Aesthetic Significance of the Face," in *Essays on Sociology, Philosophy and Aesthetics By Georg Simmel et al.*, edited by Kurt Wolff (New York: Harper & Row, 1959), p. 277.
4. Simmel, "The Aesthetic Significance of the Face," p. 277.
5. R. D. Laing, *The Divided Self* (Baltimore: Penguin, 1959).
6. Meredith Tax, "Woman And Her Mind" in *Radical Feminism*, edited by Anne Koedt, Ellen Levine, and Anita Rapone (New York: Quadrangle, 1973), pp. 23–35.
7. Atwood, *Lady Oracle*, pp. 122–23.

Chapter 10

1. Margaret Atwood, *Lady Oracle* (New York: Simon and Schuster, 1976), pp. 50–51.

Appendix III

1. Lillian Rubin, *A Woman of a Certain Age* (New York: Basic Books, 1979).

INDEX

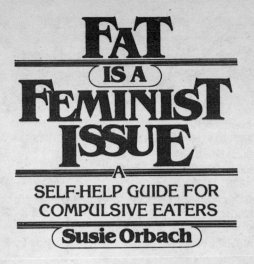

MS READ-a-thon—
a simple way to start youngsters reading

Boys and girls between 6 and 14 can join the MS READ-a-thon and help find a cure for Multiple Sclerosis by reading books. And they get two rewards — the enjoyment of reading, and the great feeling that comes from helping others.

Parents and educators: For complete information call your local MS chapter. Or mail the coupon below.

Kids can help, too!